Contents

Acknowledgements

In Britain, feminist study has had a lean time of it; so I was more than lucky to arrive at that rare institution, the Pembroke Center for Teaching and Research on Women, at Brown University. As a postdoctoral research fellow there in 1984–5, I could start off this essay; and since then it has been transatlantically encouraged by Christina Crosby and Elizabeth Weed. Thanks to a research assistantship in 1986–7 at the Institute for Advanced Study at Princeton, I could set down the reflections which the Pembroke Center had allowed me to begin.

Stephen Heath has been good enough to read closely through everything, and make useful observations. I'm grateful to him and to Colin MacCabe for their editorial backing. Especial thanks to Sarah Johns, who prepared the manuscript beautifully, and with unfailing good humour.

Nigel Wheale, whose ear doesn't fail him, offered me the quotation from *Othello* – Desdemona's question, 'Am I that name?', which is my title.

A first version of Chapter 1 appeared as an article in *New Formations*, number 1, Spring 1987: members of its editorial board, among them Homi Bhabha, Joan Copjec, and Cora Kaplan, were very helpful.

My greatest impersonal debt is to those upheavals of the women's liberation movement in Britain which evolved into the awkward, tenacious socialist feminism, feminist socialism, which has engaged, absorbed, and vexed us so much.

My overriding personal debt is to Joan Scott. I have had the extraordinary good fortune of working with her both at Brown University and at the Institute for Advanced Study at Princeton. It is impossible to make clear how much I owe to her intellectual generosity, her unwavering support, her criticism and her companionship. This essay is therefore for her, with my thanks.

DENISE RILEY

"Am I That Name?"

Feminism and the Category of "Women" in History

"Am I That Name?"

Feminism and the Category of "Women" in History

Denise Riley

University of Minnesota
Minneapolis

Published by the University of Minnesota Press
2037 University Avenue Southeast, Minneapolis MN   55414.
Published simultaneously in Canada
by Fitzhenry & Whiteside Limited, Markham.

Printed in Great Britain

Library of Congress Cataloguing-in-Publication Data
Riley, Denise (E. M. Denise)
      Am I that name? : feminism and the category of "women" in history
      Denise Riley.
          p.   cm.
      Bibliography: p.
      Includes index.
      ISBN 0-8166-1730-9   ISBN 0-8166-1731-7 (pbk.)
          1. Women—History.   2. Feminism—History.   I. Title.
      HQ1154.R55 1988   88-21640
      305.4′2′09—dc19   CIP

The University of Minnesota
is an equal-opportunity
educator and employer.

1

Does a Sex Have a History?

> *Desdemona*: Am I that name, Iago?
> *Iago*: What name, fair lady?
> *Desdemona*: Such as she says my lord did say I was.
>   (William Shakespeare, *Othello*,
>   Act IV, Scene II, 1622)

The black abolitionist and freed slave, Sojourner Truth, spoke out at the Akron convention in 1851, and named her own toughness in a famous peroration against the notion of woman's disqualifying frailty. She rested her case on her refrain 'Ain't I a woman?' It's my hope to persuade readers that a new Sojourner Truth might well – except for the catastrophic loss of grace in the wording – issue another plea: 'Ain't I a fluctuating identity?' For both a concentration on and a refusal of the identity of 'women' are essential to feminism. This its history makes plain.

The volatility of 'woman' has indeed been debated from the perspective of psychoanalytic theory; her fictive status has been proposed by some Lacanian work,[1] while it has been argued that, on the other hand, sexual identities are ultimately firmly secured by psychoanalysis.[2] From the side of deconstruction, Derrida among others has advanced what he calls the 'undecidability' of woman.[3] I want to sidestep these debates to move to the ground of historical construction, including the history of feminism itself, and suggest that not only 'woman' but also 'women' is troublesome – and that this extension of our suspicions is in the interest of feminism. That we can't bracket off either Woman, whose capital letter has long alerted us to her dangers, or the more modest lower-case 'woman', while leaving unexamined the ordinary, innocent-sounding 'women'.

This 'women' is not only an inert and sensible collective; the dominion of fictions has a wider sway than that. The extent of its reign can be partly revealed by looking at the crystallisations of 'women' as a category. To put it schematically: 'women' is historically, discursively constructed, and always relatively to other

1

categories which themselves change; 'women' is a volatile collectivity in which female persons can be very differently positioned, so that the apparent continuity of the subject of 'women' isn't to be relied on; 'women' is both synchronically and diachronically erratic as a collectivity, while for the individual, 'being a woman' is also inconstant, and can't provide an ontological foundation. Yet it must be emphasised that these instabilities of the category are the *sine qua non* of feminism, which would otherwise be lost for an object, despoiled of a fight, and, in short, without much life.

But why should it be claimed that the constancy of 'women' can be undermined in the interests of feminism? If Woman is in blatant disgrace, and woman is transparently suspicious, why lose sleep over a straightforward descriptive noun, 'women'? Moreover, how could feminism gain if its founding category is also to be dragged into the shadows properly cast by Woman? And while, given the untidiness of word use, there will inevitably be some slippery margins between 'woman' and 'women', this surely ought not to worry any level-headed speaker? If the seductive fraud of 'woman' is exposed, and the neutral collectivity is carefully substituted, then the ground is prepared for political fights to continue, armed with clarity. Not woman, but women – then we can get on with it.

It is true that socialist feminism has always tended to claim that women are socially produced in the sense of being 'conditioned' and that femininity is an effect. But 'conditioning' has its limits as an explanation, and the 'society' which enacts this process is a treacherously vague entity. Some variants of American and European cultural and radical feminism do retain a faith in the integrity of 'women' as a category. Some proffer versions of a female nature or independent system of values, which, ironically, a rather older feminism has always sought to shred to bits,[4] while many factions flourish in the shade cast by these powerful contemporary naturalisms about 'women'. Could it be argued that the only way of avoiding these constant historical loops which depart or return from the conviction of women's natural dispositions, to pacifism for example, would be to make a grander gesture – to stand back and announce that there *aren't any* 'women'? And then, hard on that defiant and initially absurd-sounding assertion, to be scrupulously careful to elaborate it – to plead that it means that all definitions of gender must be looked at with an eagle eye, wherever they emanate from and whoever pronounces them, and that such a scrutiny is a thoroughly feminist undertaking. The will to support this is not blandly social-democratic, for in no way does it aim to vault over the stubborn harshness of lived gender while it queries sexual categorisation. Nor does it aim at a glorious indifference to politics by placing itself under the banner of some renewed claim to androgyny, or to a more modern aspiration to a 'post-gendered subjectivity'. But, while it refuses to break with feminism by naming itself as a neutral deconstruction, at the same time it refuses to identify feminism with the camp of the lovers of 'real women'.

Here someone might retort that there are real, concrete women. That what Foucault did for the concept of 'the homosexual' as an invented classification just cannot be done for women, who indubitably existed long before the nineteenth century unfolded its tedious mania for fresh categorisations. That historical constructionism has run mad if it can believe otherwise. How can it be overlooked that women are a natural as well as a characterised category, and that their distinctive needs and sufferings are all too real? And how could a politics of women, feminism, exist in the company of such an apparent theoreticist disdain for reality, which it has mistakenly conflated with ideology as if the two were one?

A brief response would be that unmet needs and sufferings do not spring from a social reality of oppression, which has to be posed against what is said and written about women – but that they spring from the ways in which women are positioned, often harshly or stupidly, *as* 'women'. This positioning occurs both in language, forms of description, and what gets carried out, so that it is misleading to set up a combat for superiority between the two. Nor, on the other hand, is any complete identification between them assumed.

It is true that appeals to 'women's' needs or capacities do not, on their own, guarantee their ultimately conservative effects any more than their progressivism; a social policy with innovative implications may be couched in a deeply familial language, as with state welfare provision at some periods. In general, which female persons under what circumstances will be heralded as 'women' often needs some effort of translation to follow; becoming or avoiding being named as a sexed creature is a restless business.

Feminism has intermittently been as vexed with the urgency of

disengaging from the category 'women' as it has with laying claim
to it; twentieth-century European feminism has been constitutionally torn between fighting against over-feminisation and
against under-feminisation, especially where social policies have
been at stake. Certainly the actions and the wants of women often
need to be fished out of obscurity, rescued from the blanket
dominance of 'man', or 'to be made visible'. But that is not all.
There are always too many invocations of 'women', too much
visibility, too many appellations which were better dissolved
again – or are in need of some accurate and delimiting handling.
So the precise specifying of 'women' for feminism might well
mean occasionally forgetting them – or remembering them more
accurately by refusing to enter into the terms of some public
invocation. At times feminism might have nothing to say on the
subject of 'women' – when their excessive identification would
swallow any opposition, engulfing it hopelessly.

This isn't to imply that every address to 'women' is bad, or that
feminism has some special access to a correct and tolerable level of
feminisation. Both these points could generate much debate.
What's suggested here is that the volatility of 'women' is so
marked that it makes feminist alliances with other tendencies as
difficult as they are inescapable. A political interest may descend
to illuminate 'women' from almost anywhere in the rhetorical
firmament, like lightning. This may happen against an older,
slower backdrop of altering understandings as to what sexual
characterisations are, and a politician's fitful concentration on
'women' may be merely superimposed on more massive alterations of thought. To understand all the resonances of 'women',
feminist tactics would need to possess not only a great elasticity
for dealing with its contemporary deployments, but an awareness
of the long shapings of sexed classifications in their post-1790s
upheavals.

This means that we needn't be tormented by a choice between a
political realism which will brook no nonsense about the uncertainties of 'women', or deconstructionist moves which have no
political allegiances. No one needs to believe in the solidity of
'women'; doubts on that score do not have to be confined to the
giddy detachment of the academy, to the semiotics seminar rooms
where politics do not tread. There are alternatives to those schools
of thought which in saying that 'woman' is fictional are silent
about 'women', and those which, from an opposite perspective,
proclaim that the reality of women is yet to come, but that this

time, it's we, women, who will define her. Instead of veering between deconstruction and transcendence, we could try another train of speculations: that 'women' is indeed an unstable category, that this instability has a historical foundation, and that feminism is the site of the systematic fighting-out of that instability – which need not worry us.

It might be feared that to acknowledge any semantic shakiness inherent in 'women' would plunge one into a vague whirlpool of 'postgendered' being, abandoning the cutting edges of feminism for an ostensibly new but actually well-worked indifference to the real masteries of gender, and that the known dominants would only be strengthened in the process. This could follow, but need not. The move from questioning the presumed ahistoricity of sexed identities does not have to result in celebrating the carnival of diffuse and contingent sexualities. Yet this question isn't being proposed as if, on the other hand, it had the power to melt away sexual antagonism by bestowing a history upon it.

What then is the point of querying the constancy of 'men' or 'women'? Foucault has written, 'The purpose of history, guided by genealogy, is not to discover the roots of our identity but to commit itself to its dissipation.'[5] This is terrific – but, someone continues to ask, whatever does feminism want with dissipated identities? Isn't it trying to consolidate a progressive new identity of women who are constantly mis-defined, half-visible in their real differences? Yet the history of feminism has also been a struggle against over-zealous identifications; and feminism must negotiate the quicksands of 'women' which will not allow it to settle on either identities or counter-identities, but which condemn it to an incessant striving for a brief foothold. The usefulness of Foucault's remark here is, I think, that it acts as a pointer to history. It's not that our identity is to be dissipated into airy indeterminacy, extinction; instead it is to be referred to the more substantial realms of discursive historical formation. Certainly the indeterminacy of sexual positionings can be demonstrated in other ways, most obviously perhaps by comparative anthropology with its berdache, androgynous and unsettling shamanistic figures. But such work is often relegated to exoticism, while psychoanalytic investigations reside in the confined heats of clinical studies. It is the misleading familarity of 'history' which can break open the daily naturalism of what surrounds us.

*　　*　　*

There are differing temporalities of 'women', and these substitute the possibility of being 'at times a woman' for eternal difference on the one hand, or undifferentiation on the other. This escapes that unappetising choice between 'real women' who are always solidly in the designation, regardless, or post-women, no-longer-women, who have seen it all, are tired of it, and prefer evanescence. These altering periodicities are not only played out moment by moment for the individual person, but they are also historical, for the characterisations of 'women' are established in a myriad mobile formations.

Feminism has recognised this temporality in its preoccupation with the odd phenomenology of possessing a sex, with finding some unabashed way of recognising aloud that which is privately obvious – that any attention to the life of a woman, if traced out carefully, must admit the degree to which the effects of lived gender are at least sometimes unpredictable, and fleeting. The question of how far anyone can take on the identity of being a woman in a thoroughgoing manner recalls the fictive status accorded to sexual identities by some psychoanalytic thought. Can anyone fully inhabit a gender without a degree of horror? How could someone 'be a woman' through and through, make a final home in that classification without suffering claustrophobia? To lead a life soaked in the passionate consciousness of one's gender at every single moment, to will be be a sex with a vengeance – these are impossibilities, and far from the aims of feminism.

But if being a woman is more accurately conceived as a state which fluctuates for the individual, depending on what she and/or others consider to characterise it, then there are always different densities of sexed being in operation, and the historical aspects are in play here. So a full answer to the question, 'At this instant, am I a woman as distinct from a human being?', could bring into play three interrelated reflections. First, the female speaker's rejections of, adoptions of, or hesitations as to the rightness of the self description at that moment; second, the state of current under-standings of 'women', embedded in a vast web of description covering public policies, rhetorics, feminisms, forms of sexualisa-tion or contempt; third, behind these, larger and slower subsid-ings of gendered categories, which in part will include the sedimented forms of previous characterisations, which once would have undergone their own rapid fluctuations.

Why is this suggestion about the consolidations of a

classification any different from a history of ideas about women? Only because in it nothing is assumed about an underlying continuity of real women, above whose constant bodies changing aerial descriptions dance. If it's taken for granted that the category of women simply refers, over time, to a rather different content, a sort of Women Through the Ages approach, then the full historicity of what is at stake becomes lost. We would miss seeing the alterations in what 'women' are posed against, as well as established by – Nature, Class, Reason, Humanity and other concepts – which by no means form a passive backdrop to changing conceptions of gender. That air of a wearingly continuous opposition of 'men' and 'women', each always identically understood, is in part an effect of other petrifications.

To speculate about the history of sexual consolidations does not spring from a longing for a lost innocence, as if 'once', as John Donne wrote,[6]

> Difference of sex no more wee knew
> Than our Guardian Angells doe

Nor is it a claim made in the hope of an Edenic future; to suggest that the polarity of the engaged and struggling couple, men and women, isn't timeless, is not a gesture towards reconciliation, as if once the two were less mercilessly distinguished, and may be so again if we could stop insisting on divisive difference, and only love each other calmly enough. My supposition here – and despite my disclaimer, it may be fired by a conciliatory impulse – is rather that the arrangement of people under the banners of 'men' or 'women' are enmeshed with the histories of other concepts too, including those of 'the social' and 'the body'. And that this has profound repercussions for feminism.

It follows that both theories about the timelessness of the binary opposition of sexual antagonism and about the history of ideas of women could be modified by looking instead at the course of alignments into gendered categories. Some might object that the way to deal with the monotonous male/female opposition would be to substitute democratic differences for the one difference, and to let that be an end to it. But this route, while certainly economical, would also obliterate the feverish powers exercised by the air of eternal polarity, and their overwhelming effects. Nor does that pluralising move into 'differences' say anything about their origins and precipitations.

I've written about the chances for a history of alterations in the collectivity of 'women'. Why not 'men' too? It's true that the completion of the project outlined here would demand that, and would not be satisfied by studies of the emergence of patriarchs, eunuchs, or the cult of machismo, for example; more radical work could be done on the whole category of 'men' and its relations with Humanity. But nothing will be ventured here, because the genesis of these speculations is a concern with 'women' as a condition of and a trial to feminist history and politics. Nor will the term 'sexual difference' appear as an analytic instrument, since my point is neither to validate it nor to completely refuse it, but to look instead at how changing massifications of 'men' and 'women' have thrown up such terms within the armoury of contemporary feminist thought.

How might this be done? How could the peculiar temporality of 'women' be demonstrated? Most obviously, perhaps, by the changing relations of 'woman' and her variants to the concept of a general humanity. The emergence of new entities after the Enlightenment and their implicatedness with the collectivity of women – like the idea of 'the social'. The history of an increasing sexualisation, in which female persons become held to be virtually saturated with their sex which then invades their rational and spiritual faculties; this reached a pitch in eighteenth-century Europe. Behind this, the whole history of the idea of the person and the individual, including the extents to which the soul, the mind, and the body have been distinguished and rethought, and how the changing forms of their sexualisation have operated. For the nineteenth century, arguments as to how the concept of class was developed in a profoundly gendered manner, and how it in turn shaped modern notions of 'women'.[7] These suggestions could proliferate endlessly; in these pages I have only offered sketches of a couple of them.

What does it mean to say that the modern collectivity of women was established in the midst of other formations? Feminism's impulse is often, not surprisingly, to make a celebratory identification with a rush of Women onto the historical stage. But such 'emergences' have particular passages into life; they are the tips of an iceberg. The more engaging questions for feminism is then what lies beneath. To decipher any collision which tosses up some novelty, you must know the nature of the various pasts that have led up to it, and allow to these their full density of otherness.

Indeed there are no moments at which gender is utterly unvoiced. But the ways in which 'women' will have been articulated in advance of some prominent 'emergence' of the collectivity will differ, so what needs to be sensed is upon what previous layers the newer and more formalised outcropping has grown.

The grouping of 'women' as newly conceived political subjects is marked in the long suffrage debates and campaigns, which illustrate their volatile alignments of sexed meaning. Demands for the franchise often fluctuated between engagement with and disengagement from the broad category of Humanity – first as an abstraction to be exposed in its masculine bias and permeated, and then to be denounced for its continual and resolute adherence, after women had been enfranchised, to the same bias. An ostensibly unsexed Humanity, broken through political pressures of suffragist and antisuffragist forces into blocs of humans and women, men and women, closed and resealed at different points in different nations. In the history of European socialism, 'men' have often argued their way to universal manhood suffrage through a discourse of universal rights. But for women to ascend to being numbered among Humanity, a severe philosophical struggle to penetrate this category has not eliminated the tactical need to periodically break again into a separately gendered designation. The changing fate of the ideal of a non-sexed Humanity bears witness to its ambiguity.

*   *   *

Yet surely – it could be argued – some definitive upsurge of combative will among women must occur for the suffrage to be demanded in the first place? Must there not, then, be some unambiguously progressive identity of 'women' which the earliest pursuers of political rights had at their disposal? For, in order to contemplate joining yourself to unenfranchised men in their passion for emancipation, you would first have to take on that identity of being a woman among others *and* of being, as such, a suitable candidate too. But there is a difficulty; a dozen qualifications hedge around that simple 'woman', as to whether she is married or not, a property-owner or not, and so forth. 'Women' *en masse* rarely present themselves, unqualified, before the thrones of power; their estates divide them as inequalities within their supposed unity.

Nevertheless, to point to sociological faults in the smoothness of 'women' does not answer the argument that there must be a progressive identity of women. How is it that they ever come to rank themselves together? What are the conditions for any joint consciousness of women, which is more than the mutual amity or commiseration of friends or relations? Perhaps it could be argued that in order for 'women' to speak as such, some formal consolidation of 'men against women' is the gloomy prerequisite. That it is sexual antagonism which shapes sexual solidarity; and that assaults and counter-assaults, with all their irritations, are what make for a rough kind of feminism.

                              *   *   *

Here there is plenty of ground. We could think of those fourteenth- and fifteenth-century treatises which began to work out a formal alignment of sex against sex. These included a genre of women's defences against their vilification. So Christine de Pisan wrote 'for women' in the *querelle des femmes*. The stage was set between a sexual cynicism which took marriage to be an outdated institution – Jean de Meung's stance in his popular *Roman de la Rose* – and a contrasted idealism which demanded that men profess loyalty to women, and adhere to marriage as a mark of respect for the female sex – Christine de Pisan's position in the *Débat sur le Roman de la Rose*, of about 1400 to 1402. This contest was waged again in her *Livre de la Cité des Dames* in 1405. As the narrator, she is visited by an allegorical triad; Reason, Rectitude and Justice. It is Reason who announces to her that her love of study has made her a fit choice of champion for her sex, as well as an apt architect to design an ideal city to be a sanctum for women of good repute. This city needs to be built, because men will vilify women. Their repeated slanders stem not only from their contempt for Eve, and her contribution to the Fall, but also from their secret convictions as to the superior capacities of all women. Christine de Pisan's earlier *Épistre au Dieu d'Amours* is also couched in this protective vein.

To suffer slights in patience is the strategy recommended by this literature, which itself conspicuously does the opposite. Here submission can be a weapon, a brandished virtue secured against great odds. The more rigorous the trial, the higher the merits of the tenaciously submissive woman. Her *Épistre de la prison de vie humaine*, composed between 1416 and 1418, dedicated to Marie de

Berry, was designed as a formal comfort to women for the deaths at Agincourt of their brothers, fathers, and husbands; now these were liberated from life's long pains. But this resignation in the face of death did not eclipse sexual triumph. Christine de Pisan's last surviving work, the *Ditié de Jehann d'Arc*, was published in 1429, but written before Joan's execution; this was a song to celebrate her life as 'an honour for the female sex'.

Both the *querelles* and these other writings defend 'women' as unjustly slandered, champion heroines, and marry defiance with the advocacy of resignation, with the faith that earthly sufferings, if patiently endured, might be put to good account in the here-after. Do these ingredients make a fifteenth-century feminism the start of a long chain ending in the demand for emancipation? Certainly there are some constant features of this literature which are echoed through the seventeenth-century writings. It argues in the name of 'women', and in that it is unlike the earlier compli-cated typologies of the sexes of the works of the women mystics. The fourteenth- and fifteenth-century polemic proposes that noble women should withdraw to a place apart, a tower, a city, there to pursue their devotions untroubled by the scorn of men in the order of the world. In this, it is not far from some seventeenth-century suggestions, like those made by Mary Astell, that 'women' have no choice but to form an order apart if they want to win spiritual clarity.

Between the fifteenth- and the seventeenth-century composi-tions, what remains constant is the formal defences of the sex, the many reiterations of 'Women are not, as you men so ignorantly and harshly claim, like that – but as we tell you now, we are really like this, and better than you.' This highly stylised counter-antagonism draws in 'all women' under its banner against 'all men'. Even though its references are to women of a high social standing and grace, nevertheless it is the collectivity which is being claimed and redeemed by debate. At times this literature abandons its claims to stoicism, fights clear of its surface resigna-tion, and launches into unbridled counter-aggression. Thus 'Jane Anger', who in 1589 published a broadside, *Jane Anger her Protec-tion for Women, to defend them against the Scandalous Reports of a late Surfeiting Love*. . . . The writer, whether truly female or *agent provocateur*, burns on the page with wild rhetoric, the cry of sex against the attacking other sex, the mediaeval defences wound to the highest pitch:

Their slanderous tongues are so short, and all the time wherein they have lavished out their words freely has been so long, that they know we cannot catch hold of them to pull them out. And they think we will not write to reprove their lying lips, which conceits have already made them cocks.[8]

The retort to the surfeited lover's charges is to invert them, to mass all women against all men:

We are the grief of man, in that we take all the grief from man: we languish when they laugh, we sit sighing when they sit singing, and sit sobbing when they lie slugging and sleeping. *Mulier est hominis confusio* because her kind heart cannot so sharply reprove their frantic fits as these mad frenzies deserve.[9]

It is a litany of pure sexual outrage:

If our frowns be so terrible and our anger so deadly, men are too foolish in offering occasions of hatred, which shunned, a terrible death is prevented. There is a continual deadly hatred between the wild boar and tame hounds. I would there were the like between women and men, unless they amend their manners, for so strength should predominate, where now flattery and dissimulation have the upper hand. The lion rages when he is hungry, but man rails when he is glutted. The tiger is robbed of her young ones when she is ranging abroad, but men rob women of their honour undeservedly under their noses. The viper storms when his tail is trodden on, and may we not fret when all our body is a footstool to their vile lust?[10]

This furious lyricism is a late and high pitch of the long literature which heralded 'women' *en bloc* to redeem their reputations. Is this in any sense a precondition of feminism; a pre-feminism which is established, indeed raging, in Europe for centuries before the Enlightenment? Certainly seventeenth-century women writers were acutely conscious of the need to establish their claims to enter full humanity, and to do so by demonstrating their intellectual capacities. If women's right to any earthly democracy had to be earned, then their virtues did indeed have to be enunciated and defended; while traces of seemingly sex-specific vices were to be explained as effects of a thoughtless conditioning, an impoverished education – the path chosen by Poulain de la Barre in his *De l'Egalité des Deux Sexes* of 1673. When Mary Wollstonecraft argued that 'the sexual should not destroy the human character'[11] in her *A Vindication of the Rights of Woman*, this encapsulated the seventeenth-century feminist analysis that women must somehow disengage from their growing endemic sexualisation.

It is this which makes it difficult to interpret the defences and proclamations of 'women' against 'men' as pre-feminism. To read the work of 'Jane Anger' and others as preconditions for eighteenth-century feminism elides too much, for it suggests that there is some clear continuity between defensive celebrations of 'women' and the beginning of the 1790s claims to rights for women, and their advancement as potential political subjects. But the more that the category of woman is asserted, whether as glowingly moral and unjustly accused, or as a sexual species fully apart, the more its apparent remoteness from 'humanity' is underwritten. It is a cruel irony, which returns at several watersheds in the history of feminism, that the need to insist on the moral rehabilitation of 'women' should have the effect of emphasising their distinctiveness, despite the fact that it may aim at preparing the way into the category of humanity. The transition, if indeed there is one, from passing consolidations of 'women' as candidates for virtue, to 'women' as candidates for the vote, is intricate and obscure.

*   *   *

When the name of feminism is plunged into disgrace – for example, in Britain immediately after the end of the First World War – then the mantle of a progressive democracy falls upon Humanity; though the resurgences of feminism in the 1920s tore this apart. But before even a limited suffrage is granted, it may have to be sought for a sex in the name of a sex-blind humanism, as an ethical demand. This may work for men, but not for women. Most interesting here are the intricate debates in Britain between socialist and feminist proponents of a universal adult suffrage, and feminists who supported a limited female suffrage instead as the best route to eventual democracy; these are discussed in detail below. But what has Humanity been conjugated against? Must it be endlessly undemocratic because 'gender-blind' – or 'race-blind'? Its democratic possibilities would depend on, for example, how thoroughly, at the time of any one articulation of the idea, the sex of the person was held to infuse and characterise her whole being, how much she was gender embodied. The question of race would demand analogous moves to establish the extent of the empire of racially suffused being over the general existence of the person. A history of several categories, then, would be demanded in order to glimpse the history of one.

*   *   *

If it is fair to speculate that 'women' as a category does undergo a broadly increasing degree of sexualisation between the late seventeenth and the nineteenth centuries, what would constitute the evidence? To put clear dates to the long march of the empires of gender over the entirety of the person would be difficult indeed. My suggestion isn't so much that after the seventeenth century a change in ideas about women and their nature develops; rather that 'women' itself comes to carry an altered weight, and that a re-ordered idea of Nature has a different intimacy of association with 'woman' who is accordingly refashioned. It is not only that concepts are forced into new proximities with one another – but they are so differently shot through with altering positions of gender that what has occurred is something more fundamental than a merely sequential innovation – that is, a reconceptualisation along sexed lines, in which the understandings of gender both re-order and are themselves re-ordered.

The nineteenth-century collective 'women' is evidently voiced in new ways by the developing human sciences of sociology, demography, economics, neurology, psychiatry, psychology, at the same time as a newly established realm of the social becomes both the exercising ground and the spasmodic vexation for feminism. The resulting modern 'women' is arguably the result of long processes of closure which have been hammered out, by infinite mutual references, from all sides of these classifying studies; closures which were then both underwritten and cross-examined by nineteenth- and twentieth-century feminisms, as they took up, or respecified, or dismissed these productions of 'women'.

'Women' became a modern social category when their place as newly re-mapped entities was distributed among the other collectivities established by these nineteenth-century sciences. 'Men' did not undergo any parallel re-alignments. But 'society' relied on 'man' too, but now as the opposite which secured its own balance.

The couplet of man and society, and the ensuing riddle of their relationship, became the life-blood of anthropology, sociology, social psychology – the endless problem of how the individual stood *vis-à-vis* the world. This was utterly different from the ways in which the concept of the social realm both encapsulated and illuminated 'women'. When this effectively feminised social was then set over and against 'man', then the alignments of the sexes in the social realm were conceptualised askew. It was not so much that women were omitted, as that they were too thoroughly included in an asymmetrical manner. They were not the submerged opposite of man, and as such only in need of being fished up; they formed, rather, a kind of continuum of sociality against which the political was set.

'Man in society' did not undergo the same kind of immersion as did woman. He *faced* society, rather; a society already permeated by the feminine. This philosophical confrontation was the puzzle for those nineteenth-century socialist philosophies which contemplated historic and economic man. An intractable problem for marxist philosophy was how to engage with the question of individualisation; how was the individual himself historically formed? Marx tried, in 1857, to effect a new historicisation of 'man' across differing modes of production, because he wanted to save man as the political animal from mutation into a timeless extra-economic figure, the Robinson Crusoe advanced by some political economies.[12] But the stumbling-block for Marx's aim was its assumption of some prior, already fully constituted 'man' who was then dragged through the transformations of history; this 'man' was already locked into his distinctiveness from the social, so he was already a characterised and compromised creation.

As with man, so here – for once – with woman. No philosophical anthropology of woman can unfurl those mysteries it tries to solve, because that which is to be explicated, woman, stands innocently in advance of the task of 'discovering her'. To historicise woman across the means of production is also not enough. Nevertheless, another reference to Marx may be pressed into the service of sexual consolidations, and into the critique of the idea that sexual polarities are constant – his comment on the concept of Labour:

> The most general abstractions arise only in the midst of the richest possible concrete development, where one thing appears

as common to many, to all . . . Labour shows strikingly how even the most abstract categories, despite their validity – precisely because of their abstractness – for all epochs are nevertheless, in the specific character of this abstraction, themselves likewise a product of historical relations, and possess their full validity only for and within those relations.[13]

*   *   *

The ideas of temporality which are suggested here need not, of course, be restricted to 'women'. The impermanence of collective identities in general is a pressing problem for any emancipating movement which launches itself on the appeal to solidarity, to the common cause of a new group being, or an ignored group identity. This will afflict racial, national, occupational, class, religious, and other consolidations. While you might choose to take on being a disabled person or a lesbian, for instance, as a political position, you might not elect to make a politics out of other designations. As you do not live your life fully defined as a shop assistant, nor do you as a Greek Cypriot, for example, and you can always refute such identifications in the name of another description which, because it is more individuated, may ring more truthfully to you. Or, most commonly, you will skate across the several identities which will take your weight, relying on the most useful for your purposes of the moment; like Hanif Kureishi's suave character in the film *My Beautiful Laundrette*, who says impatiently, 'I'm a professional businessman, not a professional Pakistani'.

The troubles of 'women', then, aren't unique. But aren't they arguably peculiar in that 'women', half the human population, do suffer from an extraordinary weight of characterisation? 'Mothers' also demonstrate this acutely, and interact with 'women' in the course of social policy invocations especially; in Britain after 1945 for instance, women were described as either over-feminised mothers, or as under-feminised workers, but the category of the working mother was not acknowledged.[14] So the general feminine description can be split in such ways, and its elements played off against each other. But the overall effect is only to intensify the excessively described and attributed being of 'women'.

Feminism of late has emphasised that indeed 'women' are far from being racially or culturally homogeneous, and it may be thought that this corrective provides the proper answer to the hesitations I've advanced here about 'women'. But this is not the same preoccupation. Indeed there is a world of helpful difference between making claims in the name of an annoyingly generalised 'women' and doing so in the name of, say, 'elderly Cantonese women living in Soho'. Any study of sexual consolidations, of the differing metaphorical weightings of 'women', would have to be alerted to the refinements of age, trade, ethnicity, exile, but it would not be satisfied by them. However the specifications of difference are elaborated, they still come to rest on 'women', and it is the isolation of this last which is in question.

It's not that a new slogan for feminism is being proposed here – of feminism without 'women'. Rather, the suggestion is that 'women' is a simultaneous foundation of and an irritant to feminism, and that this is constitutionally so. It is true that the trade-off for the myriad namings of 'women' by politics, sociologies, policies and psychologies is that at this cost 'women' do, sometimes, become a force to be reckoned with. But the caveat remains: the risky elements to the processes of alignment in sexed ranks are never far away, and the very collectivity which distinguishes you may also be wielded, even unintentionally, against you. Not just against you as an individual, that is, but against you as a social being with needs and attributions. The dangerous intimacy between subjectification and subjection needs careful calibration. There is, as we have repeatedly learned, no fluent trajectory from feminism to a truly sexually democratic humanism; there is no easy passage from 'women' to 'humanity'. The study of the historical development and precipitations of these sexed abstractions will help to make sense of why not. That is how Desdemona's anguished question, 'Am I that name?', may be transposed into a more hopeful light.

2

Progresses of the Soul

And as they fled they shrunk
Into 2 narrow doleful forms
Creeping in reptile flesh upon
The bosom of the ground:
And all the vast of Nature shrunk
Before their shrunken eyes.
(William Blake, from 'Africa',
The Song of Los, 1795)

The notion of what a women is, alters; so does the whole conception of what a person is, how a being is unified. A part of this malleable ingredient of being human is the degree to which possession of a gender is held to invade the whole person. And here the critical gender is female; again, it is the difficulties of the woman-to-human transition. It is 'women' who are sexualised, it is femininity which comes to colour existence to the point of suffusion.

But this slow transition which takes place between, roughly, the seventeenth and late eighteenth centuries isn't narrowly linear. It does not so much rest on a simple hardening of the opposition of 'men' to 'women'. It is implicated in changes to concepts of the dominion of the soul over the body, and of the nature of the reasoning faculties. In the broad traditions of Christian theology, even though woman's being may be dangerously close to the body, carnality is not restricted to the feminine, and the soul is relatively unscathed by its sex. But a newer and relatively secularised understanding of that person – in particular the woman, who became an ambulant Nature – represents a differently constructed ensemble altogether. The gradual processes of secularisation and theological revision were accompanied by an increasing sexualisation which crowded out the autonomous soul – while at the same time a particularly feminised conception of Nature began to develop. The slow loss of the sexually democratic soul was the threat to late seventeenth-century forms of feminism in particular. At the same period as these religious transformations, the influence of Cartesian philosophy entailed a sharp conceptual distinction between mind, soul, and body. Given that the idea of woman, throughout as before the Renaissance, continued to occupy a special proximity to the body and carnality, Cartesianism could only implicitly underwrite her greater remoteness from the mind. So seventeenth-century philosophical suppositions did nothing to impede the renewed sexualisation of the female intellectual capacities – at a time when the older theological convictions about the gender-indifference of the soul, at least, were themselves crumbling. Mind and soul remained distinguished, as the soul became more confined as an entity to the contested internal premises of a formal theology. Yet on the other hand, religiosity – the idea of intensive religious observances and piety, tarnished with sentiment and excess – became more unambiguously feminised from the late seventeenth century onward. The gross effect of these changes, taken together with others well outside of philosophy or faith, was to blur together elements which had previously been held apart into a simplified personification of woman.

In these circumstances, what is in operation is more profound and less easily classifiable than any straightforward revision of conceptions of woman. We could almost say that a new density or a new re-membering of 'women' had gradually developed, although it is true that the filiations which comprise it can be to some extent unravelled backwards. Yet they will not necessarily consist of strands clearly marked as pertaining to 'women'. The history of sexual apartheid is frequently extremely uneven. An apparently reiterated sexual antagonism may well *not* be the result of a descending line of hostilities, but be an echo of mutations of other ideas which are less easy to hear, because they have fallen away from our thought.

So to meditate about how the gendered subject is consolidated can draw one into vast areas of speculation, removed from the pressing preoccupations of feminism now. There is the whole consolidation of the human subject, and how and where the demarcations of the feminine fall. On this dizzying scale, even the ancient philosophy and theology known to the West would be 'ethnocentric' and restrictive fields of enquiry. But as alternatives to paralysis in the face of the magnitude of the task, small stabs at reapprehending partial existing histories are, at least, beginnings.

*   *   *

To classical philosophy, one could put a short but complicated question. Does the soul have a sex? Or does sexed being confine itself to the body, and if so, is there a permanent risk that it may seep through into the neutral soul? The Homeric psyche was a faint and squeaking ghost, an asexual bat-like thing which sought the shadows. The Orphic soul came of an untainted and undifferentiated celestial origin. The Platonic soul, however, passed through several scattered conceptions in its author's deliberations. It was torn, and became increasingly torn. Less and less could it be the home of any serene rationality. Thus the soul which is described in *The Republic*, and rethought elsewhere, is variable, unstable and full of internal conflicts, while in the *Phaedrus* the desires that rock it are terrible, savage, and irregular.[1] The Platonic body is in general, as in Pythagorean and Orphic belief, the tomb and the prison-house of the soul, and from it creep disorders and corruptions. Love, as Eros in the *Symposium*, is the child of the god Plenty and the goddess Poverty; like his mother, he will always suffer distress. And like a modern Lacanian, he is vexed by longings, insatiability, and repetition. The Platonic soul is divided between desires which cannot be reconciled; it is in the grip of appetites and of reason, which are set at odds with one another since appetites, which are quintessentially irrational, must be subdued by reason, which is right. Eros, the desire for what is not yet possessed, is poised between love and longing; the object which Eros seeks must be good; for it to be longed-for is not enough. Plato's tripartite soul, thus imperilled in its own recesses, does not itself possess a gender and the formal equality of the souls of men and women is not raised as a question. The associations of the rational elements in the soul, nevertheless, are with metaphors of maleness while the irrational is proximate to the intemperate pursuits of the flesh.[2]

Successive convictions of the closeness of woman to the sensual body makes the theoretical neutrality of the soul an imperilled but tenacious attribute in the history of Christianity. Augustine's sexual asceticism, indeed his horror, is celebrated enough; yet he championed the spiritual equality of women against their diminished rationality. The mind, according to Augustine, knows no sex; yet the mind's intimacy with the body opens it constantly to the risk of being stained. When the eye of the mind is distracted from the eternal, when 'the light of its eyes is not with it', such clouding may well be caused by earthly carnality. When the identification of the sensual with the bodies of women in particular is fully established and when the desiring subject is understood to be male, then the souls of women can only become vestigial hiding-places of innocence which remain under a permanent threat of invasion and contamination by their flesh. The old Pauline antithesis of soul and body, the imperative to master sensuality for the redemption of the soul, was not gender-specific and did not of itself bring about the equation of women's bodies with a corrupt carnality, and women's souls with diminished spiritual capacities. But it was built on the risk of that association: a risk which, sensed, was vigorously contested.

For both the fullness of the souls of women and their propensity to be driven by sexual longing are themes which persist in the writings of women of the middle ages. The Abbess Hildegard of Bingen, who was born in 1098 and died, famous for her prophecies, judgement, and scholarship, in 1179, wrote works of theology, physiognomy, and medicine. These included a series of characterologies; the sex and the temperament of a child, she held, was the outcome of the time and the physiology of its parents' lovemaking, which she elaborated in her *Causae et Curae*. Here the four humours are described for both women and men. The melancholic woman, for example:

> But there are other women who have gaunt flesh and thick veins and moderately sized bones: their blood is more lead-coloured than sanguine, and their colouring is as if it were blended with grey and black. They are changeable and free-roaming in their thoughts, and wearisomely wasted away in affliction; they also have little power of resistance, so that at times they are worn out by melancholy. They suffer much loss of blood at menstruation, and they are sterile, because they have a weak and fragile womb. So they cannot lodge or retain or warm a man's seed, and thus they are also healthier, stronger, and happier without husbands than with them – especially because, if they lie with their husbands, they will tend to feel weak afterwards. But men turn away from them and shun them, because they do not speak to men affectionately, and love them only a little. If for some hour they experience sexual joy, it quickly passes in them.[3]

The existence of such elaborated typologies make is clear that 'carnality' is hardly a simple or self-evident notion for either sex.

Certainly, as Peter Dronke's commentary suggests,[4] the writings of Hildegard of Bingen are sometimes shadowed by the Manicheanism of an always-flawed sensuality, the gloomy inheritance of the Fall:

> The soul is a breath striving towards the good, but the body strives towards sins; and rarely and at times hardly at all can the soul restrain the body from sinning; just as the sun cannot prevent little worms from coming out of the earth to the place that he is warming in his splendour and heat.[5]

But in her meditations this antithesis is transient and irregular, and a lyrical physiology is also prominent:

> When a woman is making love with a man, a sense of heat in her brain, which brings with it sensual delight, communicates the taste of that delight during the act and summons forth the emission of the man's seed.[6]

Occasional flickerings of Manichean thought notwithstanding, her writing never espouses what a later terminolgy might describe as a female nature. There is no equation of 'women' *tout court* with a dangerous sensuality which religious observance must restrain; nor yet with the naïve sexualisation of religious longing. Another student of theology, the celebrated Heloise who died in 1163, was far from holding sensuality to be a disgrace; it was to be examined, and the degree of austerity appropriate to religious women was arguable.

Other women mystics disprove the charge of an uniquely female ecstasy. Marguerite Porete, a Beguine, was executed on a charge of heresy at Paris in 1310. She was seized by the vision of a Holy Church as a union of free souls: near the final stages of earthly liberation, the Sacraments and churchmen were not essential for salvation, and unmediated contact with God was also possible. Blinded, she believed, by their own desires and will, and their own fear, conventional churchmen were impervious to Love as the pure image of Plenitude. Yet for Marguerite Porete, as for Plato in the *Symposium*, that Love remains in a constant high tension with its own need. She 'dreams the King',[7] dreams of the fable of Alexander and the maiden and thus of direct access to the God she loves and imagines for herself. In her aristocracy of divine Love, there is no blissful passivity; spiritual aspirations do not entail the renunciation of the body. In her *Le Miroir des Simples Ames*, written sometime between 1285 and 1295, she describes a struggle:

> The heart all alone waged this battle over him, and it answered in anguish of death that it wanted to abandon its love, by which it had lived.[8]

An ambiguous passage in which the sense of the ferocity of feared loss, at least, is unmistakable. Between the twelfth and the four-teenth centuries, mystical writers, men and women, laboured over and refought the requirements of their faith for asceticism. It is not that 'women' were fully consigned to the body, or that a unique hysteria characterised the woman mystic. A continuum of sensual and spiritual ecstasy was at the least a possibility for both sexes; while struggles between flesh and spirit, where these were felt to be at war with each other, were not the prerogative of men alone. The religiosity of a swooning female passivity, the eroticised icon most familiar to us in Bernini's rendering of St Theresa, is a later interpretation which reviews the mystic writers with a sardonically sexualising eighteenth-century gaze.

Still, it would be more misleading to assume that the earlier period was generously free of the hierarchies of sex; it's a matter of the changing dominions and territorial annexations which pre-sented themselves for, in shorthand, sexualisation. The perennial question here is almost one of emphasis; is continuity or discon-tinuity to be traced; are we to wonder bitterly at the fertile proliferations or subordination of 'women', or seize with modified optimism upon evidence of deep differences in the forms of sexualising? Some historians of the sixteenth century have stressed a kind of ideological lag where matters of gendered stratification lay. There was, suggests Ian Maclean, less of a change in the whole notion of women throughout the Renaissance than the intellectual upheavals and new studies of that period might lead one to look for; 'at the end of the Renaissance, there is a greater discrepancy between social realities and the current notion of woman than at the beginning'.[9] The Aristotelian conception of woman which had continued to permeate Renaissance thought was abandoned, by medicine and physiology at least, by 1600. Nevertheless, this did not entail the end of the thinking which consigned her to a lower stratum of being, even if that being could now be understood as undistorted in itself:

> Although she is thought to be equally perfect in her sex, she does not seem to achieve complete parity with man, or does so only at the expense of considerable dislocation in medical thought. Her physiology and humours seem to destine her to be the inferior of man, both physically and mentally.[10]

So the associations of deprivation with the differences of sex persisted, in an altered form. The old Aristotelian conceptions had posited imperfection within herself as the mark of woman, and translated into mediaeval understanding these emerged as 'deprived, passive, and material traits, cold and moist dominant humours and a desire for completion by intercourse with the male'.[11] Women themselves were the result of a generative event which was never completed; necessary though they were for the survival of the human species, individually each was by definition imperfect; and imperfect in the etymological sense too, of not fully carried through. This theory of woman as a misbegotten male, as if interrupted in a trajectory, could imply that woman was at once a kind of systematic exception and not necessarily of the same species as man. Indeed an anonymous work of 1595 enquired as to whether women are or are not human.[12] But such works were, as Maclean demonstrates, produced as jokes against some other object, and although the question, 'Is woman monstrous?' was voiced, its tone was always satirical or facetious. The very imperative of difference for the continuation of the species saved woman from the serious attribution of monstrosity. She must be a creature which accorded with 'the general tendency of nature (intentio naturae universalis)' whereas monsters had to be created by some truly unnatural disposition.[13] Aristotle's own *Metaphysics*, moreover, held that men and women could not be assigned to different species. The *Metaphysics* rehearsed what it believes to be the old Pythagorean oppositions, including that of male to female; but then Aristotle set out to produce more complex theories of these and other oppositions. There could be difference of privation ('species privata') as well as differences of relation – and to be female could embody both forms. The balance retained a systematic if altered idea of the inferiority of women throughout the Renaissance. In Maclean's summary,

Renaissance theology and law reflect in the main a conservative view of sex, linking it to the opposite of privation and to contrariety. In ethics and medicine, the 'species relativa' is more in evidence, and one may detect a continuum of change rather than discontinuity. But even in these disciplines, the conservative view of sex difference survives, and causes notable dislocations of thought, especially where psychology is in question. Underlying this Aristotelian taxonomy of opposition are Pythagorean dualities, which link, without explanation, woman with imperfection, left, dark, evil and so on. These emerge most obviously in medicine, but are implied in theology and ethics also.[14]

Nevertheless, theology did hold out a limb of significant hope. Even if the morality of woman were questionable, and her assignation to the cold and moist humours undermined her emotional control and her reasoning powers, since these were associated with warmth and dryness, all was not lost:

Most writers suggest that woman is less well endowed with moral apparatus, and continue the practice of praising saintly women for their paradoxical virtue. But, like woman's subordination to her husband and her disqualification from full participation in the spiritual life, this inequality is attached to this life only, and all commentators stress that she will share equally in the joys of paradise. In theological terms, woman is, therefore, the inferior of the male by nature, his equal by grace.[15]

*   *   *

This formula set the overshadowing agenda for the flurries of sixteenth-century feminist polemic which irrupted in Europe, and it continued to be crucial for seventeenth-century feminisms too. It was imperative to hang on to the conception of the equality of spiritual grace, while conceding as little as possible to the conception of nature's dominion. Some pursued this argument within the radical religious associations and faiths, as Quakers especially; the Civil War sects in the 1640s and 1650s provided useful debating platforms, however transiently. Others, differently placed, laboured to demonstrate their intellectual powers as guarantees of their claims to egalitarian standing. Some women authors achieved a scholastic flamboyance; the prolific writings of Margaret, Duchess of Newcastle, ran splendidly wild over the terrain of human knowledge known to her. In one dramatic piece,[16] she uses the figure of a 'she Anchoret', a female oracle who holds forth confidently to the various flocking audiences come to solicit her opinions on science, business, morality, religion, marriage and education. The Anchoret is also given to pronouncements on the natural and historical worlds alike, and here the Duchess displays a fine lyricism in her definitions of natural phenomena: light was 'inflamed air', the moon 'a body of water', snow 'curdled water', hail 'broken water', and frost, 'candied vapour'. But tyranny defeats high style, for the She Anchoret commits a principled suicide rather than endure a forced marriage into a neighbouring kingdom or else precipitate a war by her refusal.

The same nympholepsy is the stuff of her *Orations of Divers Sorts, Accomodated to Divers Place*, of 1662. Here the Duchess has composed both sides of debates on subjects of a political and ethical hue. Among her great range of topics of seventeenth-century contention, she has a section entitled Femal Orations. Thesis and antithesis are set out in pairs. One set of orations proposes the sufferings of women at the hands of men, then counter-proposes what men do for women, who would, it claims, otherwise be helpless in the world. Another set debates the most apt penalties for adultery, against the permissibility of divorce on the grounds of cruelty. There are two pairs of debates which are devoted to contrasting modes by which women might ascend to some measure of power. Ought they to 'imitate men' and refuse the assignations held fitting to their sex – or would it be more prudent to rely instead on the exercise of the traditional 'feminine virtues' which were able to enslave men by discreet means? So the first debater within this set emphasises the emptiness of 'women' thus:

> Let us Hawk, Hunt, Race and to the like Exercises as Men have, and let us Converse in Camps, Courts, and Cities, in Schools, Colleges, and Courts of Judicature, in Taverns, Brothels and Gaming Houses, all which will make our Strength and Wit known, both to Men, and to our own Selves, for we are as Ignorant of our Selves, as Men are of us. And how sheuld we Know our Selves, when as we never made a Trial of our Selves? or how should Men know us, when as they never Put us to the Proof? Wherfore, my Advice is, we should Imitate Men, so will

our Bodies and Minds appear more masculine, and our Power
will Increase by our Actions.[17]

The antithetical argument sets aside this tactic of borrowing the
armour of the opposers, for fear of ending up in a no-man's and a
no-woman's land:

> We cannot change the Nature of our Sex, for we cannot make
> ourselves Men; and to have femal Bodies, and yet to Act Mas-
> culine Parts, will be very Preposterous and Unnatural; in Truth,
> we shall make our Selves like as the Defects of Nature, as to be
> Hermaphroditical, as neither to be Perfect Women nor Perfect
> Men, but Corrupt and Imperfect Creatures.[18]

The better tactic, then, would be to pursue the feminine virtues, to
become 'Modest, Chast, Temperate, Humble, Patient and Pious:
also to be Huswifely, Cleanly, and of few Words'.[19]

The next pair of Orations elaborate the struggle towards equality
on the one hand, and the insistence on the natural superiority of
women within their differences on the other:

> Since all terrestrial Imitations ought to Ascend to the Better, and
> not to Descend to the Worse, Women ought to imitate Men, as
> being a degree in Nature more Perfect, than they Themselves,
> and all Masculine Women ought to be as much praised as
> Effeminate Men to be Dispraised, for the One advances to
> Perfection, the other Sinks to Imperfection, that so by our
> Industry we may come at last to Equal Men both in Perfection
> and Power.[20]

To this the former speaker retorts that such sentiments do
unnecessary violence, in that they

> perswade us out of our Selves, as to be That, which Nature
> never Intended us to be, to wit Masculine, since our own Sex
> and Condition is for the Better.[21]

For the dangers and travails of men would serve to age and
damage women, and 'Destroy their Tender Lives' needlessly.
Women possess their own natural gifts which force the love and
desire of men, and thence their enslavement: 'and what can we

Desire more, than to be Men's Tyrants, Destinies and God-
desses?'.[22]

Here are the polarities of the mid-seventeenth-century arguments; their familiarity is conspicuous and their repetitions need
no emphasis. Yet what sense can we make of this very familiarity
of the sexual oppositions set out formally here? The Duchess of
Newcastle organised them in their ranks as evidence of her mastery of this as of a myriad other rhetorical debates. It is hard to read
them lightly, or as mere displays of technical virtuosity. With the
intermittent bitterness, there's a weariness; it's as if the alignment
of sex against sex can find very few expressive forms and must
soon lapse into monotony, reiterations of the old *querelles*.

By the end of the century, new arguments make their appearance. The author of *An Essay in Defence of the Female Sex*, which
was published anonymously in 1696, attacks the tedium of the
literature of sexual wars. Vigorously setting herself against the
temptation to make easy alliances, she refuses to follow the example of 'Mr W' (possibly Wycherley) whose championing of her
sex is somewhat ambiguous: he

> thinks us sufficiently fortified, if out of the story of Two
> Thousand Years he has been able to pick up a few examples of
> Women illustrious for their Wit, Learning or Vertue, and Men
> infamous for the contrary: though I think the most inveterate of
> our Enemies would have spar'd him that Labour, by granting
> that all Ages have produc'd Persons famous or infamous of both
> Sexes: or they must throw up all pretence to Modesty, or
> Reason.[23]

The author herself resolves not to scrabble for Great Women
through the ages, and writes firmly that she

> shall leave Pedants and School-Boys to rake and tumble the
> Rubbish of Antiquity, and muster all the Heroes and Heroins
> they can find to furnish matter for some wretched Harangue, or
> stuff a miserable Declamation with instead of Sense or Argu-
> ment.[24]

Nor will she submit herself to the strictures of those critics of her
writing who declare that her style is too masculine:

But, with their leave, I think I may boldly advance, that let them form themselves with equal care, by the same Models, and they will no more be able to discern a Man's Stile from a Woman's, than they can tell whether this was written with a Goose Quill, or a Gander's.[25]

The author first passionately dismisses the notion that writing, and hence thought, can be sexually aligned; there are no 'woman's voices'; and indeed her *Essay in Defence of the Female Sex* is remarkable in the lineage of defensive literature because it is largely antipathetic to championing female virtues. Instead it scrutinises differences which result from social custom. It is the wordly circumstances of men, their education, their 'Freedom of Converse'[26] which gives them the edge of advantage, yet may not the conversation of women also profit ingenious men? There are some savants, she says, who maintain that there is 'no such distinction, as Male and Female Souls'.[27] The body may indeed be able to influence the mind, yet bodily differences are not pertinent: 'I see therefore no natural Impediment in the structure of our Bodies'.[28] Nor does the natural world teach any damning lessons on this score: 'in Brutes and other Animals there is no difference betwixt Male and Female in point of Sagacity'.[29]

[handwritten margin note: do rabbis think men & women have dif. souls?]

Neither the body nor nature can account, she considers, for the subjugation of women. Nor can any simple conception of society; for there are clear differences among the estates and sometimes these may be fairly egalitarian in their treatment of women. Among country labouring people, she observes, 'the Condition of the two Sexes is more level, than amongst Gentlemen, City Trades, or rich Yeomen'.[30] She knows too that Dutch women handle business affairs themselves, and that this is considered nothing remarkable.

Later a suspicion of sex-specific virtues darts into the author's analysis: women are conspicuous for their 'Vivacity' and their 'Readiness of Invention'; 'we were chiefly intended for Thought, and the Exercise of the Mind' whereas men must use their vaunted strength on 'action and labour'.[31] Jealous of their gifts of quickness, men, writes the anonymous author in a familiar vein, oppress women out of envy. Yet she proceeds with an elaborate series of arguments which have no interest in natural attributions; social causes can be found, she insists, for apparent sexual differ-

ences. We may ignore with justice the historians' evidence about
the natural basis of the legal suppression of women: 'for if any
Histories were anciently written by Women, Time, and the Malice
of Men have effectually conspir'd to suppress 'em'.[32]

Girls are put at a disadvantage, for, educated apart after the age
of six or seven, they lack a training in the classics. Yet even this
need not be an insurmountable handicap, for translations abound,
most prominently by Dryden. There are enough fine works composed originally in English by poets, critics, moralists, essayists
like Locke, dramatists. Yet why, she wonders, are there so few
works by women authors, with the honourable exceptions of a few
like Mrs Philips and Mrs Behn? Because, she believes, potential
women writers may be thwarted at the outset, persuaded by
custom

> never to enquire so far into themselves and their own Abilities,
> as to bring such a thought into their Heads. This last I fancy is
> the true Reason, why our Sex, who are commonly charged with
> talking too much, are Guilty of writing so little.[33]

Vanity and incompetence are vices generously scattered
throughout the population of men, too; she digresses to satirical
denunciations of the Pedant and the Country Squire among
others, to attacks on the Beau, the Bully, the Poetaster, the
Coffee-House Savant and the tedious breed of Natural Historians,
'Vertuoso's' who never know when to subside. Such men are
indeed better dissemblers, having enjoyed a sophisticated school-
ing in the arts of dissimulation; and they are more racked by envy
and ambition, vices which have a greater scope to flourish in that
sex which most perambulates the social world. That the
capabilities of women for wisdom are less exercised and
developed is an effect of their upbringing: but, the anonymous
writer adds, the earlier maturing of sense in girls is universally
acknowledged: the judgment of a fifteen-year-old girl may well
equal that of a twenty-one-year-old youth.

All these have the ring of arguments familiar in a later feminism.
Not nature, but culture, is the cause of the apparent deficiencies of
women. The female subject is what she is made. What she is, is
not known. As Margaret, Duchess of Newcastle wrote, 'we are as
Ignorant of our Selves, as Men are of us'. Or, as the Cartesian
reformer, Poulain de la Barre, had suggested in 1673, no innate

inferiority could sensibly be deduced from the past performances
of women who lacked education. Successive nineteenth-century
feminisms made similar propositions – John Stuart Mill would
echo them in his *The Subjection of Women* of 1869 – but the
particular vexation and spur of seventeenth-century feminism is
the status of the soul as it relates to the increasingly sexed self. If
woman – who is not known – becomes more and more assigned to
the natural order in which human custom merely follows instinct,
then that indeterminate self, which education might prove and
clarify, also suffers a trivialising contraction. Only the spiritual
equality of women stood in the way of a thoroughgoing and
reductive feminisation. This was under serious threat, however;
to find new grounds for egalitarian argument was imperative. The
plea for education intensified.

One of the best-known seventeenth-century advocates of
women's emancipation by means of education, Mary Astell, was a
High Church Tory and the author of anti-dissenting works. Her *A
Serious Proposal to the Ladies, for the Advancement of their True and
Greatest Interest* of 1694 proposes a version of Christine de Pisan's
city of ladies. How are enforced, not innate, incapacities to be
remedied?

> We will therefore enquire what it is that stops your flight, that
> keeps you groveling here below, like Domitian catching Flies
> when you should be busied in obtaining Empires.[34]

Let women, she pleads, only be given equal opportunities for
religious studies, not in order to usurp male dominions, but for
the salvation of their own souls: 'Our only endeavour shall be to
be absolute Monarchs in our own Bosoms.'[35] To this end, let
women go to a 'Religious Retirement' and there learn to

> Disengage our selves from all our former Prejudices, from our
> Opinion of Names, Authorities, Customs and the like, not give
> credit to any thing any longer because we have once believ'd it,
> but because it carries clear and uncontested Evidence along with
> it.[36]

By such means the chances of spiritual redemption will not be
jeopardised by the imposed distractions of 'tinselware' on earth.
Later she turns her attention to the lot of those women who are

already entrenched, by the exercising of their own impoverished choices, within worldly institutions. Her *Some Reflections upon Marriage*, of 1700, is an extraordinary piece of writing. Its surface of piety and devotion to the idea of educating women to a due understanding of their duty is constantly ripped across by the most bitter irony, which at times seems to run beyond the author's control. How, she asks, should women properly submit themselves and bear the worldly frustrations of their hope?

> A Prospect of Heaven, and that only, will cure that Ambition which all Generous Minds are fill'd with; not by taking it away, but by placing it on a right Object.[37]

In this Heaven the venerable traditions of spiritual democracy will be triumphantly fulfilled: 'her Soul shall shine as brightly as the greatest Heroe's' to compensate it for those repeated injuries inflicted by the 'Customs of the World'.[38]

But while she is on earth, then adherence to her duty must demand her education to that duty:

> Superiors don't rightly understand their own Interest when they attempt to put out their Subjects Eyes to keep them Obedient. A Blind Obedience is what a Rational Creature shou'd never Pay, nor wou'd such a one receive it did he rightly understand its Nature.[39]

Mary Astell goes on to systematically explode the case she has been advancing, and turns around her own injunctions to the virtue of an informed submission in marriage thus: why should a woman marry, and endure the mortification of her own will for a husband who may not deserve this? Such a marriage would indeed be a kind of martyrdom which would need the most rigorous education in firmness of purpose for the woman. For if you chose to marry a tyrant, once the tyranny has been made plain to you, it will only cause you to be more refractory. Not that there is any even distribution of guilt in a union made unhappy by such a husband; 'both Parties are indeed Guilty, but the Aggressors have a double Guilt, they have not only their own but their Neighbours ruin to answer for'.[40]

She allows the duty of women's submission within marriage, only in order to lay it at the feet of Custom or of religious duty – as

The question - is the "inferiority" of women seen as inherent or social?

Progresses of the Soul 33

opposed to any notion of Natural Inferiority. From whence then, she asks, come the worldly disadvantages of women? Not from divine or from natural disposition. Social practice is the culprit; girls are 'restrain'd, frown'd upon, and beat, not *for* but *from* the Muses: Laughter and Ridicule, that never-failing Scare-crow, is set up to divert them from the Tree of Knowledge'.[41]

Mary Astell's astringent advocacy of the virtues of reserve, discretion and constancy in wives is matched by her insistence that, however much obedience to a brutish husband may be praiseworthy, the wife had better choose cautiously in the first place:

> She who elects a Monarch for life, who gives him an Authority she cannot recall however he misapply it . . . had need be very sure that she does not make a Fool her Head, nor a Vicious Man her Guide and Pattern, she had best stay till she can meet with one who has the Government of his own Passions, and has duly regulated his own Desires, since he is to have such an absolute power over hers.[42]

Yet is it reasonable, she implies, to demand such maturity of judgment from a woman who has been systematically mis-educated? For women's training has served

> to disturb, not to regulate their Passions; to make them timorous and dependent, and in a word, fit for nothing else but to act a Farce for the Diversion of their Governours.[43]

Again she argues that it's a cruelty to reproach women for those shortcomings which men force upon them, and a cruelty to demand their submission to that which they can't fully understand, then to ascribe their incomprehension to their integral nature. The battle against characterisations of women's nature is already joined. Mary Astell is well aware of how categories of 'women' can be used in the service of contempt. On the one hand, she writes:

> Women are nor so well united as to form an Insurrection. They are for the most part wise enough to love their Chains and to discern how very becomingly they sit. . . . Let them in short be what is call'd VERY Women, for this is most acceptable to all

sorts of Men; or let them aim at the Title of Good Devout
Women, since some men can bear with this.[44]

The determination to *be* a woman, to live into the expectations
aroused by the categorisation, has its uses. Yet even this, she
argues, affords no reliable protection:

> But how can a Man respect his Wife when he has a contemptible
> opinion of her and her Sex? When from his own Elevation he
> looks down on them as void of Understanding, and full of
> Ignorance and Passion, so that Folly and a Woman are equival-
> ent terms with him?[45]

Such sexual antagonism can cut two ways:

> We who made the idols, are the greater Deities: and as we set
> you up, so it is in our power to reduce you to your first
> obscurity, or to somewhat worse, to Contempt.[46]

The reign of antagonisms offers an inhuman prospect, though:
'Contempt is scarce a human passion.'[47] Nevertheless, even the
sentiment of scorn towards women might serve as a disguised
generosity to the sex, if it woulf only serve to activate them, to
wrench them into protest against

> the whole design of those fine Discourses which have been
> made against the Women from our great Fore-fathers to this
> present Time![48]

Again and again this writing sets up a surface of measured
serenity, but shatters it. Only in God can sexual difference be
finally transcended. On this earth there is no settled happiness,
even though some divinely sanctioned concessions did exist:

> God himself who is no Respecter of Persons, with whom there is
> neither Bond nor Free, Male nor Female, but they are all one in
> Christ Jesus, did not deny Women that Divine Gift the Spirit of
> Prophecy, neither under the Jewish nor Christian Dispensa-
> tion.[49]

In a manner perhaps more familiar to modern readers from Mary
Wollstonecraft's *A Vindication of the Rights of Women* of almost a

century later, Mary Astell reiterates that in so far as women display
faults of character, these are the *débris* of a silly and pernicious
education, and from them nothing about women's 'natural' disposition could be fairly deduced. Careful distinctions must be
drawn, she insists repeatedly, between the natural potential and
the socially crippled capacities of women. Here an education in
self-knowledge is the key. As she writes in *Reflections upon Marriage*:

> For Sense is a Portion that God himself has been pleas'd to
> distribute to both Sexes with an Impartial Hand, but Learning is
> what Men have engross'd to themselves, and one can't but
> admire their great Improvements![50]

No appeals to Nature are to be allowed where they mask the
inflictions due to Custom; and where the democracy of the soul
can be claimed, then Mary Astell deploys the arguments from that.
Her insistence that the defects of femininity are taught, and that
what 'women', undistorted, might be is unknown, is constantly
supported by the premise of a native spiritual equality. In this
respect, feminism after Mary Astell has a worse foe to contend
with once concepts of Nature have risen to the fore so as to
envelop 'women' utterly.

*   *   *

The many directions from which new assertions about the natural
were pronounced had little in common bar a lack of progressive
implications for thinking about the sexes. If secular theories of
human nature in general tended to underwrite the relation between men and women and to emphasise sexual difference,
theological debates about the possibility of salvation again
returned to the proximity of sexuality to the fall from grace. In the
mid eighteenth-century religious controversies in France which
preceded the expulsion of the Jesuits, Jansenists, anti-humanist
and ascetic, looked back to an Augustinian view of the corruptible
character of human nature. They attacked, in the name of a
rigorous and unflinching anti-humanism, what they saw as the
indulgences of the more leisurely Jesuitical attitude to earthly life,
which foresaw at least the possibility of redemption for all; as
Pascal said, only some were allowed efficacious grace by God
while the rest of mankind dwelt in the provenance of concupis-
cence.[51] The darkness of the soul underwent an increasing sexual-

isation in theological thought in England after the Restoration, while the later languages of natural right in the secular world were largely unperturbed by the soul, and saw societal arrangements as Custom sensibly sanctioning Nature. This set the terms of the polemic – what was ascribable to innate differences, and what to the inroads of habit and education. As the possibilities of arguing from the natural democracy of the soul fell away, the associations of 'women' with the natural were magnified to a point of mutual implication.

Rousseauesque thought is the readiest example of this. There is nothing to be gained from setting about the ears of Rousseau himself – that he offers no comfort to feminism is well enough established, as are the idiosyncracies of his positions. Still, it can be safely claimed that Rousseau's notoriously complicated version of human nature did entail a high degree of sexualisation of that nature: the infusion of the state of being a woman with a 'woman's' nature so that no neutral enclave of the person remains unfilled and unoccupied by femininity.

La Nouvelle Hélöise, first published in 1761, the elaborate account of a romance conducted in letters, offers substantially the same antipathies to the rights of women as those advanced in Émile a year later. This would be the gloomy inheritance for Mary Wollstonecraft, as it was the fruition of Mary Astell's intimations as to the horrors of appeals to women's nature. In the drama 'the moral distinction between the sexes'[52] is played out fully. As a participant in it writes:

> The soul of a perfect woman and a perfect man ought to be no more alike than their faces. All our vain imitations of your sex are absurd; they expose us to the ridicule of sensible men, and discourage the tender passion we were made to inspire.[53]

The pupil Émile lives under a system of intimate tutelage which amounts to voyeuristic surveillance, most exaggerated in the narration of his courtship and marriage to Sophie. For a wife, fidelity to Nature demands uncritical submission; not because any spiritual consolations may be looked for, but because here Nature is the fixed hierarchies of the social order. Women are the embodiment of this ordered Nature, so that disturbances of the natural practices of maternity, for instance, will have monstrous consequences. The young Sophie 'should be as truly a woman as Émile is a man' – she must posses all those characteristics of her sex which are required to enable her to play her part in the physical and moral order. 'But for her sex, a woman is a man; she has the same organs, the same needs, the same faculties.'[54]

Yet what does Rousseau mean by the sex of a woman? He himself is hesitant in his very assertiveness:

> General differences present themselves to the comparative anatomist and even to the superficial observer; they seem not to be a matter of sex; yet they are really sex differences, though the connection eludes our observation. How far such differences may extend we cannot tell.[55]

Yet again he confidently states, as in *La Nouvelle Héloïse*, 'A perfect man and a perfect woman should no more be alike in mind than in face.'[56] So the 'sex' of the woman is in fact a generally suffusing characteristic. Hence the difference in the temporalities of gendered being for men and for women, periodicities which Rousseau names, but doesn't remove from the realms of mass psychology: 'The male is only a male now and again, the female is always a female, or at least all her youth; everything reminds her of her sex.'[57] The thesis that 'The native characters of sex should be respected as nature's handiwork'[58] launches a long polemic against contemporary notions of the rights of women, for

> Women do wrong to complain of the inequality of man-made laws; this inequality is not of men's making, or at any rate it is not the result of mere prejudice, but of reason.[59]

'The general laws of nature and morality'[60] entail that childbearing is the lot of women, and where they are defied in other spheres, as with Plato's stipulations in *The Republic* that the wives of Guardians should be trained as the men, chaos ensues:

> that political promiscuity under which the same occupations are assigned to the sexes alike, a scheme which could only lead to intolerable evils; I refer to that subversion of all the tenderest of our natural feelings, which he [Plato] sacrificed to an artificial sentiment which can only exist by their aid.[61]

The seekers after rights, women usurpers,

fall below their own level as women, instead of rising to the
level of men . . . Do not try to make your daughter a good man in
defiance of nature. Make her a good woman, and be sure it will
be better for both her and us.[62]

This, in the teeth of

our modern philosophy which makes a jest of female modesty
and its so-called insincerity. I also perceive that the most certain
result of this philosophy will be to deprive the women of this
century from such shreds of honour as they still possess.[63]

It is as if a strongly conventional identity of 'women' must be
maintained in order to secure the identity of 'men'. Indeed,
Rousseau says that whereas 'The poor may come to manhood
without our help'[64] nevertheless the achievement of men's social-
sexual capacities demands, as its precondition, that women be
women:

Would you restore all men to their primal duties, begin with the
mothers: the results will surprise you. Every evil follows in the
train of this first sin; the whole moral order is disturbed, nature
is quenched in every breast, the house becomes gloomy, the
spectacle of a young family no longer stirs the husband's love
and the stranger's reverence.[65]

There's no doubt that the prior identification of one sex allows that
of the other: 'When women become good mothers, men will be
good husbands and fathers.'[66] The necessary conservatism of
sexual identifications, where 'women' bear such a heavy responsibility for securing the proper order of things, emerges again in
that complementary consciousness Rousseau ascribes to the sexes.
Reason overshoots the feminine and in so doing characterises it,
and its own implicit maleness. Women, embedded in natural
wisdom, still lack the self-reflexivity of rationality.[67] Though they
may function passively as moral texts in their existence, they are
by definition devoid of the powers of analytic thought.

There is the implication in Rousseau that, if human nature
possesses a history and is eminently social, then it is capable of
amelioration. As Alasdair McIntyre comments:

It is one of Rousseau's cardinal virtues to have asked for an explanation of specific ills in human life, and in so doing, to have opened the way for sociological hope to replace theological despair.[68]

This general will to the common good, shorn of Hobbesian cynicism and of spiritual Manicheanism, needed some new expression of the generality of citizens. But how could the impossible sexual democracy of the citizen ever be reached, if women were barred by Rousseau to being claimants to political subjecthood? 'Sociological hope' is the expression of the sociological collectivity, with all its fragilities, and it was this which came to challenge, in the name of political emancipation, the emptiness of the generality which obscured it.

* * *

How could woman ever become a rational and therefore a potentially political subject, given the powers of her assignation to the natural which in the Rousseauesque schema sustains the very social order at its best? Madame de Staël, almost forty years after the publication of *Émile*, meditated on the curiously transitional state of her sex in *De La Littérature*:

> The rank which women hold in society is still, in many respects, indeterminate . . . in the present state of things they are placed neither in the order of nature, nor in the order of society.[69]

Woman, she surmised, was a hybrid being who lived in the uneasy condition of the freed slave; 'helotism' was the term which best spoke for her condition. Vexed herself by torments of self-consciousness which, she held, must afflict the 'exceptional' woman, the woman as writer, Madame de Staël described the plight of those who may come to regret their prominence:

> sense, talents, an impassioned mind, may induce them to emerge from the cloud in which they ought always to be enveloped: but they never cease to recur to it with regret as their safest asylum.[70]

For whatever the true isolation of the woman writer, her existence as such must always expose her to the cruelties of gossip. Yet how,

she wondered, might the feminine 'virtues' be retained while it
was nevertheless necessary to overstep the boundaries set by
convention in search of a genuine independence of thought? She
concluded her book with an agonised dilemma: the struggle
between reasoned and affective expression, where the terms were
all dictated by notions of femininity:

> By what means can a distinction be made twixt the talents and
> the mind? How can we set aside what we feel, when we trace
> what we think? how impose silence on those sentiments which
> live in us, without losing any of the ideas which those senti-
> ments have inspired? What kinds of writings would result from
> these continual combats? Had we not better yield to all the faults
> which arise from the irregularities of nature?[71]

Madame de Staël's burst of despair is indeed comprehensible;
while passion and emotion must fight it out within the language of
the woman writer who was caught in the grip of conventions
which stressed an apposite femininity, there could be little hope
for any progressive resolution. On the contrary, the growing
eroticising of 'women' diminished such possibilities severely. As
Ian Watt has suggested:

> It is, in all events, very evident that the eighteenth century
> witnessed a tremendous narrowing of the ethical scale, a re-
> definition of virtue in primarily sexual terms.[72]

If virtue was to be assessed on a restricting compass of the sexual,
and the whole being of women *was* their sex which was so
proximate to sexuality, then women as pretenders to the ethical
were radically handicapped in their very existence. The ethical
sphere was hardly democratic if ontology barred its entrance thus.
If post-Rousseau woman was marked by her closeness to Nature,
that too implied her intimacy with the sexual. The whole moral
potential of women was therefore thoroughly different, and their
relation to the order of moral reason was irretrievably not that of
men's. Ethics has a history, and the history of women as ethical
subjects unfolds along contorted paths of alliance with the idea of
nature, and with the later idea of the social.
    Hegel was quite clear on this. Writing about the family in the
Phenomenology of the Spirit in 1807, he locates the internal family

emotions as the unconscious notion of the ethical, as opposed to the family's full ethical status as a part of the community or Society. The link towards that universality is the father, who moves also in the outer world; the virtuous woman, the wife, must work with the realm of the natural, the domestic, and the particular, which will always drag her backwards. Hers is a different, yet none the less authentic, order of ethical being from that offered by the civic world. Again, the sister's relation to her brother possesses a distinctive ethical quality, which is familial but unmixed with sexual emotion. Both the Hegelian wife and sister occupy distinct and virtuous niches in the home. Thus the two sexes acquire 'the significance of their respective determinations'.[73] But universal ethical life may only be achieved by the citizen who is able to move in the communal world outside the private household: the man. There is for Hegel no conception of woman *tout court* as an ethical being; she is intelligible only within her various immersions in the family. How, then, may the woman ever cross over into society, and ascend to the condition of the fully social individual? If women are only to be thought *in relation*, then the status of being a woman while being a social-ethical subject is a logical impossibility. There are analogous difficulties for the Kantian scheme of ethical being; there the moral agent must have a strict autonomy, must function as a sovereign individual. Women, always conceived in relation, are therefore impossible as subjects.

As for ethics, so for politics. The attainment of the natural right to liberty after the late seventeenth century was intimately bound up with the ownership of property; Locke's state of nature was both familial and property-holding. And if, from the aspect of both ethical theory and their ascribed natural disposition, women's habitat was that familial sphere, however might women, without property, ever begin to lay claim to political subjecthood? If women's natures are indeed increasingly sexualised in the course of the eighteenth century – on top of their deep implausibility as ethical and political actors – then the inheritance of obstacles to the development of feminism is indeed monstrous. As the soul of the woman shrinks and is made gender-specific, so vice swells in her body; not, of course, with any novelty, except that, crucially, the territorial powers of the body are at the same time enlarged.

Intimate, particular, familial, pre-rational, extra-civic, soaked in its sexual being; a femininity thus understood needed to be

shored up against its own risks of overflooding its walls.
Threatened vagaries of sexual identities preoccupy several
eighteenth-century writers. As one of Clarissa Harlowe's corres-
pondents writes to her, describing a vigorous housewife who had
crossed into the domains of the stud servants, 'Indeed, my dear, I
do not think a man-woman a pretty character at all.'[74] If it was
probable that there was some continuity between the nature of a
man and that of a woman, where were the boundaries? A woman
who resembled a man, like the old woman who haunts the scene
of the main crime in Richardson's Clarissa, had a uniquely night-
marish and unspeakable caste. She exemplified a hybrid nature,
which was not simply 'masculine' and therefore susceptible at
least to analysis, but was indescribable. Diderot too discusses the
mongrel 'homme-femme'. His Sur les Femmes of 1772 dwells on the
play of the female reproductive cycle, and on an invalidism which
marks out the entire being of the woman, such that her whole
condition is also pathological; 'it seems that Diderot regards
femininity as a kind of permanent hypnosis', observes Rita Goldberg.[75] Woman, her femininity displayed on the level of her very
writing and speech, has become virtually an embryonic
psychiatric classification.

Richardson's Clarissa is a clear example of a sexualised religiosity which is being deployed in order to scrutinise religious conviction. Goldberg has suggested that it is the trial of a young woman
on the ground of sexuality, made as a test of the social world in
which she moved; 'The history of misreadings of Clarissa is one
clue that it was regarded as a test of beliefs about both religion and
sexuality.'[76] There is indeed nothing unprecedented about the
conviction that there are close proximities between the spiritual
and the erotic, exemplified by the mediaeval mystics of both sexes.
But a different phenomenon altogether occurred when the slow
extension of a homogenising Nature, aided by independent revisions in theological thought, pervaded the idea of the soul of
woman so as to displace it. These changes were allied to a literary
sensualising of women's religious adherence. Together they contributed powerfully to a largely stultifying formation in which a
definitive and relentlessly internally consistent 'women's nature'
was established and named.

In this long process, those appeals to the ungendered soul which
had provided such useful platforms for seventeenth-century
feminists, religious radicals and reformers, Quakers and members

of Civil War sects, became anachronisms.[77] Those versions of spirituality which the nineteenth century elaborated were generally given to asserting the distinctively 'womanly' soul in which the supposedly highest qualities of femininity were refined; the very characterisation of this sexed soul was not contested. That the soul before God had no sex was not an argument available for feminist deployment after the eighteenth century's revisions of Nature and Reason. It was not merely that ideas about women had changed. The whole meaning of 'woman' had been transformed once the concept of the female person as thoroughly sexed through all her regions of being had become entrenched. As the neutral domains of the soul had contracted, so it had become possible to *be* a sex.

3

'The Social', 'Woman', and Sociological Feminism

Susan B. Anthony (voice from behind the statue):
It is a puzzle, I am not puzzled but it is a
puzzle, if there are no children there are no men and
women, and if there are men and women, it is rather
horrible, and if it is rather horrible, then there
are children, I am not puzzled but it is very
puzzling, women and men vote and children, I am
not puzzled but it is very puzzling.
> (Gertrude Stein, libretto for
> *The Mother of Us All*, an operetta
> by Virgil Thomson, 1947)

Writing in the first year of the nineteenth century, Madame de Staël lamented the inheritance of chaotic Republican notions of women allied to the devastations bequeathed by Rousseauesque suppositions. She reflected:

The education of women has, in all free countries, been adapted to the peculiar constitution established in each: at Sparta they were accustomed to the exercise of war; at Rome, austere and patriotic virtues were required of them. If, therefore, it is wished that the principal object of the French republic should be emulation in mental improvement and philosophy, it would surely be a rational plan to promote the cultivation of the female mind, in order that men may find companions with whom they may converse on subjects the most interesting to themselves. Nevertheless, since the revolution, men have thought it politically and morally desirable to reduce the female mind to the most absurd mediocrity: the conversation they have addressed to women, has been in a language as devoid of delicacy as of sense; and consequently the latter have had no inducement to excite the powers of their understanding.[1]

44

If this continuing abasement of women was propelled by a fear
that men could only become full Republicans at the cost of sacrific-
ing women's best characteristics, this was a sad misapprehension:

> During the course of the revolution, those same women have
> given the most numerous and convincing proofs of energy and
> intrepidity. Frenchmen can never become such absolute repub-
> licans, as wholly to annihilate the independence and pride
> natural to the female character.[2]

It followed, as it had for Mary Wollstonecraft, that women
should be educated, and that their improvement would benefit
everyone:

> If the condition of the female world in the civil order of things is
> very defective; surely to alleviate their situation and not to
> degrade their mind, is the order most desirable. Assiduously to
> call forth female sense and reason, is useful both to mental
> improvement and the happiness of society.[3]

A new object, society, could be proposed as the beneficiary of
female education, something at once stronger and less precise than
the good of 'men' or women's spiritual redemption. If the post-
revolutionary goal was the restitution of some natural nobility,
then that social object, Madame de Staël insisted, could only be
damaged if the range of education was narrowed:

> It is not by contracting the sphere of ideas, that the simplicity of
> the primitive ages can be restored; and the only result of such a
> system is, that less understanding has produced less delicacy,
> less respect for public opinion, and fewer means of supporting
> solitude.[4]

Madame de Staël's unhappiness was not be be resolved. Not
only were women, after the Revolution, doomed to suffer 'sol-
itude' in their previous darkness, but the empire of Nature continued to swell. It dictated or at least sanctioned not only a
restricted education, but the terms of succeeding decades of eman-
cipationist debate in Europe. For instance, that strange hybrid of
an expression, 'natural rights', sounds as if it might have held
open a door to the claim for political rights. Yet this could not

happen without some revision of 'the natural', and this came
surprisingly late. For a century at least, Nature flourished, among
other places, within the argument for 'separate spheres' which so
tormented the suffrage debates; women's natural differences contributed to their fixation within the domestic realm. In 1869, John
Stuart Mill was only able to echo the older emancipationists'
argument as it had been raised in the eighteenth century: that any
appeals to the self-evident forms of women's destiny under the
sway of Nature must be empty, because Nature only presents itself
in an already distorted shape:

> If men had ever been found in society without women, or
> women without men, or if there had been a society of men and
> women in which the women were not under the control of the
> men, something might have been positively known about the
> mental and moral differences which may be inherent in the
> nature of each. What is now called the nature of women is an
> eminently artificial thing – the result of forced repression in
> some directions, unnatural stimulation in others.[5]

Harriet Taylor (Mill), writing in 1851, constructed her lucid pleas
for liberation from 'the aristocracy of sex' by emphasising the
contingency of supposedly gender-innate behaviour. She alluded
to Sydney Smith's persuasion that sexual differences can be
explained through the effects of circumstances alone, 'without
referring to any conjectural differences of original conformation of
mind'.[6] To demand both educational and civic enfranchisement
entailed, as Harriet Taylor's essay demonstrated, a rigorous critique of the reigning conviction that women possessed a thoroughly
distinct mentality.

But this was not the end of the task: some means of endowing
'women' with compensatory characteristics was also necessary to
assert them as likely candidates for emancipation. How might
'women' be, in effect, rehabilitated? If the legacy of the eighteenth
century had been an intensification of a naturalised femininity,
placed firmly in the family, then it's *as if* these very ascriptions
were taken on in the nineteenth century, to be wielded as
weapons of women's elevation. If woman's sphere was to be the
domestic, then let the social world become a great arena for
domesticated intervention, where the empathies supposedly
peculiar to the sex might flourish on a broad and visible scale. If

'women' were a separate species, then let them make a separate contribution to the world, and let their efforts humanise the public. If the subjection of women had been secured by their very designation as 'women', then let that be seized and, refashioned, set to work. Even their alleged 'conformation of mind', in Harriet Taylor's phrase, might be usefully deployed at one level, while it was denied at others. Certainly, all this was an effect, rather than a strategy. And all of this was heavily dependent on the formulation of the new sphere of 'the social'.

*   *   *

Both this 'social' and 'women' lean forward, as concepts, into a future which is believed to sustain them. It is as if 'women', who have been erroneously or ignorantly represented, might yet, reconstructed, come into their own. In many later nineteenth and indeed early twentieth-century addresses on the Woman Question, they are caught up not in being, where they are massively misunderstood, but in becoming. If 'women' can be credited with having a tense, then it is a future tense. It is true that the trajectory of 'man' in the nineteenth-century human sciences often winds him backward to the riddles of his origins, or alternatively, reels him out towards the double question of his ends, in the senses of his purposes and his extinction.[7] But nineteenth-century 'women' do not suffer so much from uncertainty about their teleology – but rather about their realisation. What might they become; what might they not become?

The very durability of this imaginative projection of a time for and of 'women' bears witness to its power. Indeed it echoes through feminisms today; the Future can still be Female. In this returning and visionary narrative, that new space which fully-realised women will come to occupy will be transformed by them to the good. This prospect lent itself to adaptation by socialist moralities in the nineteenth century. Fourier, for instance, envisaged the transition of women towards a full humanity, an ascendant flight which would shed its light on all; Marx echoed Fourier's conviction that how any society treated its women was an index of its real civilisations; Engels repeated the idea of women as true bearers of the moral future – they inhabited and embodied those moral standards to which men, too, would in time aspire under socialism; and Owen looked for the establishment of that New Moral World in which women would come into their own. 'Women', for these socialisms, functioned as an anti-positivist spiritual category, in the very decades when new forms of positivism developed.

There was nothing innovatory about the conception of women as improvers. Some Enlightenment theorists had advanced their own versions of it; Millar's *Origin of the Distinction of Ranks* in 1771 had included 'women' as indices of civilisation, as a kind of social leaven.[8] Other forms of installing them in society were more problematic. Although Quesnay in his *Tableau Économique* of 1758 had produced a model of class which effaced them as economic actors, earlier theories, including Quesnay's own, had not done so.[9] The economic assignation of 'women' continued to be uncertain, but their status as elevating agents was simpler and less troubling. The development of concepts of class generally perpetuated the familiar bifurcation of 'women': into 'human', the aspect which was tractable for theorisation, and into 'different', the aspect which was notoriously less so.

What did change the concept of 'women' by furnishing it with a new terrain was not so much class, which multiplied the old ambiguities as it refurbished them, but 'the social'. This harnessed the supposedly less ambiguous spiritual capacities of 'women' to fresh ends. At the same time, it could deal with the tarnished associations of 'women' by affecting a bland redistribution and dilution of the sexual onto the familial. Or it could settle the irresistibly sexualised elements of 'women' onto new categories of immiseration and delinquency, which then became sociological problems. This new production of 'the social' offered a magnificent occasion for the rehabilitation of 'women'. In its very founding conceptions, it was feminised; in its detail, it provided the chances for some women to enter upon the work of restoring other, more damaged, women to a newly conceived sphere of grace.

Auguste Comte went out of his way to emphasise the connection he saw between his new sociological science and 'women'. In his *A General View of Positivism*, of 1858, he was confident that those who would most readily embrace and profit from his work would be those very groups which lacked a stake in maintaining the status quo:

It is among women, therefore, and among the working classes that the heartiest supporters of the new doctrine will be found

. . . Having but little influence in political government, they are the more likely to appreciate the need of a moral government, the special object of which it will be to protect them against the oppressive action of the temporal power. It is from the feminine aspect only that human life, whether individually or collectively considered, can really be comprehended as a whole.[10]

Such largesse of comprehension, Comte believed, stemmed from

That subordination of intellect to social feeling; a subordination which we find directly represented in the womanly type of character, whether regarded in its personal or social relations.[11]

And indeed, it was the feminist Harriet Martineau who translated Comte's first course of lectures, as *The Positive Philosophy*.[12]

This shining projection of 'women' alights on a newly conceived space which is deeply caught up in allied peculiarities. The nineteenth-century 'social' is the reiterated sum of progressive philanthropies, theories of class, of poverty, of degeneration; studies of the domestic lives of workers, their housing, hygiene, morality, mortality; of their exploitation, or their need for protection, as this bore on their family lives too. It is a blurred ground between the old public and private, voiced as a field for intervention, love, and reform by socialists, conservatives, radicals, liberals, and feminists in their different and conjoined ways. Like the modern collectivity of 'women', it carries an air of natural good sense; yet both in their mutual references can be traced to a complicated post-1790s gestation.

Once the seemingly neutral and vacant backdrop of 'the social' presents itself for scrutiny, it appears as a strange phenomenon in its own right. This is another matter from that familiar questioning by today's social historians as to the 'ideological' deployments which are carried out in the name *of* the social. On the contrary, once the authenticity of 'the social' is called into question in itself, it cannot function as a neutral site upon which progress or reaction may win the day. Instead we could look critically at what Jeffrey Minson has called 'The ideal of the social as a secular greater-than-that-which-cannot-be-thought'[13] – as a potential earthly heaven which is open to the play of perpetual transformability because of its very apartness from the individual who is 'in' it.

The ubiquitous 'social' as the groundswell of the Western world offers a total geography for comprehension and reform. 'Women' and other sociological categories, arrayed in groups, stretch out 'in' this vast space. They are embedded in a new topography, which does not have a conscious past. So they are figures in a landscape, rather than episodes in a history. Yet the spatiality of the new 'social' of the nineteenth century also resonates with the grandly anti-positivist 'woman' who antedates all sociology. Many mysticisms conceive of the feminine, the maternal body, as an archaic space. The Platonic *chora*, which is prior to all metaphysics, is, in its endlessness, curiously reminiscent of the new 'social'. In the *Timaeus* it is

> Indefinitely a place; it cannot be destroyed, but provides a ground for all that can come into being; itself being perceptible, outside of all sensation, by means of a sort of bastard reasoning; barely assuming credibility, it is precisely that which makes us dream when we perceive it, and affirm that all that exists must be somewhere in a determined place.[14]

One of the peculiarities of 'women' in its proximity to 'the social' is a doubled feminisation. In so far as the concerns of the social *are* familial standards – health, education, hygiene, fertility, demography, chastity and fecundity – and the heart of the family is inexorably the woman, then the woman is also solidly inside of that which has to some degree already been feminised. The 'social' does not merely admit women to it; something more constructive than a matter of entry or access is going on; it is as if 'women' become established as a new kind of sociological collectivity. 'Women' both come under and direct the public gaze in the later nineteenth century as sociological subjects in a double sense. Studies of poverty and of family life, of 'social conditions', are from the 1880s to the 1930s frequently explained as the ravages of deprivation on the family whose pivot and heart is 'the working-class woman', she who may also be represented as its ignorant saboteur. In France the 'social question' has earlier associations with militant socialism; in Britain it becomes synonymous somewhat later with a broad anxiety about the intimate conditions of working-class domestic life: nutrition, budgets, household management, maternal morbidity, infant mortality, child neglect, wage-earning women and their dependents. This closeness of 'women' and 'the social' is then refined and underwritten by philanthropic, feminist and women's labour associations, who frequently understand themselves, *qua* women investigators, to be apt investigators and managers of the plight of the 'working-class woman'. Women contribute enormously to the studies of 'women'. This observation isn't made to undermine the usefulness and seriousness of the often scrupulously detailed work done in the name of a progressive politics, by the Fabians, for example; but to emphasise the fact that 'women' became both agents and objects of reform in unprecedented ways with the ascent of the 'social'.

One striking effect of the conceptualising of this 'social' is its dislocation of the political. The latter takes on an intensified air of privacy and invulnerability, of 'high politics' associated with juridical and governmental power in a restricted manner. The question of poverty, for instance, becomes divorced from politics and assigned, especially in the work of the French political economists, to the social sphere. The associations of 'women' with this sphere accompany a displacement and a permanent erosion of older distinctions between the 'public' and the 'private', at the same time as the constriction of the 'political' is refined. 'Women' are overwhelmingly sociological and therefore, given these new definitions, not political entities; indeed the suffrage struggles grind on in vain during these decades, as emancipation is endlessly deferred. Political parties and their adherents develop 'the social'; feminism follows the same course. The social is in this sense constructed, rather than being the universal agent which bathes everything else. The more progressive and humanitarian the aspirations of politics and philanthropy, the more determinedly and exhaustively 'the social' is shaped, wielded, and scrutinised in the later nineteenth century. As it alters conceptions of the terrain of politics, it becomes a subdued key to the nature of political theory. As it is engaged with feminism, embracing women encapsulated 'in' the family, 'in' society, so it simultaneously shapes the nature and history of modern feminism.

*   *   *

Certain feminist organisations could work with and through the discourse of 'the social', not to undermine it radically, but to make some differentiations within its smoothness, and to try, tacitly, to reinsert its political implications. Their efforts might labour against accepted wisdoms to demonstrate the innocence of the 'working-class mother' from the fecklessness with which she was publicly charged; to lay bare the real precariousness and monotony of life on 'round about a pound a week' or to expose the sufferings of those women in childbirth and childrearing. The Fabian Women's Group carried out the most elaborate surveys to argue for the needs of working-class women; the Women's Co-operative Guild publicised loss and deprivation as well as solidarity.[15] A whole train of liberal and socialistic investigations begun in the 1890s continued with renewed energy in the post-war period, reinforced by innovations in sociology.[16] The celebrated closeness between liberalism and sociology has received critical attention from historians, yet the oddities of the whole rise of 'the social', into which women-in-the-family are so knitted, have largely escaped unnoticed. It's as if 'women' comprise a school of natural objects for this 'social'.

Indeed the British organisation for the promotion of a then embryonic sociology, the National Association for the Promotion of Social Science, prided itself on its capabilities to enfold both working men and women. Its *Transactions* describe its 1858 second annual general meeting where 'the policy and management of Trades Unions were debated with the assistance of several working men',[17] culminating in a public meeting at Queen's College. Here there was

a great gathering of some thousands of working men and women in the amphitheatre, in which the leading members of the Association and several artisans took part.[18]

Such phenomena were evidence, to the National Association, of

a daily increase of sympathy and support from all quarters. The papers contributed by working men to the Liverpool meeting give a fair promise of adherence from a class whom the Association has endeavoured, from the commencement, to enlist in its rank . . . the number of the gentler sex among our list of authors is one sign among others that women are beginning to exercise a more active influence for social improvement.[19]

These authors included some luminaries who were hardly at the beginning of their philanthropic careers: Mary Carpenter, writing on Ragged Schools; Louisa Twining on Workhouse Visiting

Societies; Mary Ann Baines on the Ladies National Association for the Diffusion of Sanitary Knowledge; and Florence Nightingale on the construction of hospitals, with her own architectural plans for improvements. Was there, indeed, some of them wondered, a special contribution of 'women' to such fields? Louisa Twining was prepared to widen the net further:

> Kind hearted people there may have been here and there, but no systematic efforts have yet been made, as they might be, to reclaim from still lower depths of degradation the sick, the sinful, and the outcast of our parish work-houses. Such a work remains for us to do, and though we have called it essentially one for women to enter upon, we would not by any means limit it to them, but earnestly invite the co-operation of all who have the time to devote to it.[20]

Mary Ann Baines, on the other hand, was convinced of the uniquely didactic powers of educated women to raise the moral condition of the working classes by means of improvements in hygiene; an effect 'brought about through the natural relation that exists between the physical state and the moral condition'.[21] Special teaching institutions might, she thought, be established to instruct schoolmistresses and pupil teachers 'belonging to any schools for the working classes'. Here child management might flourish with few holds barred to the imperative of sound experiment: 'In order to make this part of the instruction thoroughly practical, some orphan infants will be reared in the institutions.'[22]

Louisa Twining lectured on workhouse reform under the banner of the National Association for the Promotion of Social Science; social science congresses throughout the 1860s returned to the theme of young women in workhouses. Women philanthropists, making a slow transition to their later status as social workers, acted upon and for women of the working classes under the auspices of 'social science'. And where the special influences of woman were not being brought to bear on the impoverished of England, they might be deployed in reforming the Empire. *Social Science*, the journal of the National Association, carried a letter in 1866 commending Mary Carpenter's interventions here; for she

> in her suggestions to the Governor General of India, and in her address at the Chambers of the Social Science Association, has

shown the vast field for noble work which lies open to English-women in the needs of our Indian Empire. As she has so graphically shown, while the home of the Hindoo continues what it is, the efforts made to raise him in morals and civilisation are thrown away, and that on the education of the women depends the moralisation, as it has been termed, of the whole race . . . The Government of India appears anxious to afford every aid to furthering any well devised scheme for bringing intelligent Englishwomen to help in raising the moral standard of the Hindoo female, and this plan, while carrying out the Government principle of non-interference in the religions of the nations, appears one of the most likely to be successful.[23]

So social science might formalise the elevation of 'women'; women of one degree would act upon women of a lower class, or of a different race, with a consequent moralisation of all. The hopes of philanthrophy were thus swept up and systematised. But this virtuous apartheid of 'women' only extended its terrain as the realms of the 'social' became more professionally described and demarcated. Did not this very formalisation of the goodness of 'women' to draw other and less blessed 'women' into a grand collectivity do something to ease, for instance, the suffrage arguments into acceptability? Could philanthropy not slip towards emancipation through the portals of social science?

One writer in *Blackwood's Magazine*, at least, feared that this might be so. Describing the 1861 social science congress in Dublin, he satirised the pretensions of sociology towards politics that he detected there:

We believe we are called upon to discuss not privileges but 'rights', for 'social science', we understand, takes as one of its bases the equal rights of women side by side with man . . . It is evident that we are entering on a new epoch in the world's history, and it will, we are sure, be to the lasting glory of the 'National Association' that in the great temple of the social science niches have been provided for the ladies.[24]

At Dublin, however, the spectre of female speakers was a little assuaged, for 'women proved themselves somewhat unfit for oratory, in the simple incapacity of making themselves heard'. The writer drew sardonic comfort from the limits of the new sociology's influence:

And we rejoice to think that thousands and tens of thousands of
such women may still be found, who have not given an ear to
social science or political philosophy. Yet we cannot, as we have
said, but feel that our notions on these subjects are every day
growing more out of date.[25]

Certainly *Social Science* published the writings of Mrs Bodichon
and Emily Davies on suffrage and education. In 1866 the journal
reproduced two franchise petitions to the House of Commons for
limited suffrage 'to unmarried women and widows on the same
conditions on which it is, or may be, granted to men'.[26] But the
degree of intimacy between the National Association for the
Promotion of Social Science and the suffrage lobby can't really be
characterised as a simple advocacy of women's rights. How
'women' might become candidates for translation from the social
to the political sphere depended not only on how 'women' were
conceived, but on how the understandings of those spheres themselves were altered. Their mutual dislocations produced a distinctively modern feminism. In this, a militant use of the collectivity
'women', which had hardly been possible under a sexualised
conception, became more plausible once the 'social' had produced
a proper field on which female goodness could be exercised. The
new senses of 'women' allowed their candidacy for humanity new
assault routes upon it. The older democratic appeal for equality,
based on the idea of 'rights', had cut less ice: it remained to be
seen how successful the newer appeals might prove.

* * *

If the eighteenth century had left the category of 'women' in need
of some vast renovation, then certainly the idea of citizenship
could lend itself to many broadly progressive and sanitary adapta-
tions of 'women'. Fabian thought especially seized on citizenship
as a form of political responsibility. 'The community' became an
imminently political terrain of women, a necessary funnel to
socialism, and a place for education. Mabel Atkinson, a member of
the Fabian Women's Group, wrote in 1914:

it becomes clear that the only path to the ultimate and most deep
lying ends of the feminist movement is through socialism, and
every wise feminist will find herself more and more compelled
to adopt the principles of Socialism. But the wise socialists must
also be feminists. The public spirit of willingness to serve the

community which will be necessary if the Socialist principles are to work must be inculcated into children from their earliest days. Can they be so inculcated by women who know nothing of the activities of the world beyond the four walls of their homes? Women, too, must be citizens and fully conscious of the privileges and duties of their citizenship if socialism is to be attained. Not least among the duties of that citizenship should be what Plato long ago demanded of his women guardians, that they should bear children for the service of the State.[27]

The companion of this managerial socialism, which to modern ears has sonorously fascistic and Stalinistic resonances, was a theory of the degradation of the working-class family through the ravages of capitalist inhumanity. The fascination of Fabians and other progressives, socialists, radicals, and liberals, with the worsening deformations of the family were not overspills from humanitarian charity alone; they derived from analyses of history by thinkers as diverse as Ruskin, Morris, Marx, and Engels. For Fabianism, a rational feminisation of the social sphere might restore much of what had been lost to the working-class family. So it was not only managerial, but was fired too by a nostalgic and restitutive impulse. At this broad point, not only Chartist and marxist but also Tory and 'country' critiques of the distorting savagery of capital towards the natural affections had long been able to conjoin.

Women in the working-class family were solidly buried in the sphere of reform and episodically examined there by socialistic discourses. In the unfolding of late-nineteenth-century socialist concern as it described the immiseration of the proletariat, the demarcation of the wrongs endured by women was sharp. Yet depictions of resistance to immiseration from the 1830s and 1840s onward remained roughly masculine. Understandings about 'women' had a life of their own which preceded their importation into socialist speech, and produced tensions of relocation there. Arguments on behalf of 'the working-class woman' did not necessarily rely on any tradition of class language. Those long intense campaigns to ease her lot, waged in the 1920s and 1930s by the Women's Co-operative Guild, drew more on the inheritance of the first Fabians' formulations about need than on a distinctively and self-consciously class-based rhetoric. There is frequently some noticeable independence between a socialist feminism diction about working women, and class language 'in general': it is not that we see an Adam's Rib state of affairs, whereby the woman is drawn directly out of the class description to be exposed to socialist analytic view. As elaborate as the formations of 'the working class' itself, the formations of 'the working woman' pass through other channels. If the concept of class has its sociological elements, so does its female counterpart, but her affinities with the social are differently aligned. 'The working-class woman' is a strange hybrid. How she stood in relation to both feminism and concepts of class became more obscure as sociology and social policy after the First World War became differently concentrated upon her.

In debates about public housing, that great dream of post-war reconstruction, 'working-class women' were in no way merely the female section of their class. As 'women', their femininity filled a distinctive space; it overflooded 'class'. When the housing needs of workers after 1918 were argued, it was on behalf of a body of fighting men who had returned home, to whom a just reward was due from an indebted nation. Shame would ensue if the genuine need of this working class were to be neglected, while any flickers of insurrectionism would be doused by its satisfaction. But 'working-class women' entered the housing debates not only as somewhat tarnished domestic angels, but also as the points where 'society' could best endeavour to meet the threatening and threatened class in its intimate form. At the same time, the lacks in 'the social' could be reformed: hence the inclusion of members of the Women's Labour League and other women's organisations in the drafting of municipal housing specifications and the minutiae of progressive domestic architecture prescribed in the Tudor Walters report of 1918.[28]

The 'special contribution' of the experienced woman's gaze into and out of the social was solicited for post-war planning. While the survival of feminism as such after 1918 was attacked as crudely and lamentably partisan, as an archaic individualism for a sex which failed to understand its duty to the common democratic good, 'women' infused their special areas. The internal arrangements of the home, the efficacy of the kitchen, the woman housing manager, and the woman writer on policy, all contributed to suggest that housing became for a while virtually 'a woman's subject'. This happened to an extent which outran the rationalisation that the home was where most women's days were, after all, spent. The metaphor of the woman in the home as a 'worker', albeit unpaid, was useful for the women's labour organisations to try to bargain from; but, recuperable for conservative uses too, it would run aground in the wake of invocations of 'the mother' between the wars.

Social policy focused more and more on 'the mother' as it concentrated on the family; she became more accountable for the adequate socialisation of her children and the prevention of mal-nourishment or delinquency. In the 1930s the unemployed working-class man was seen as emasculated within his family. But the woman as a mother was understood not to be in a relationship, but to be pursuing an occupation. The battle for women's organ-isations then became the exoneration of 'the working-class mother' from charges of fecklessness. She had to be moral, had to shine to avoid the charges of ignorance and bad budgeting level-led at her. In the 1920s Marion Phillips, on the executive of the women's section of the Labour Party, had spoken of the need 'to bring the mother spirit into politics'; to feminise the public sphere thus is a recurrent ambition, but one capable of being voiced from many political positions. 'The working-class mother' could be embedded in the most stultifying discourses, as pro-natalist rhetoric in Britain after 1939 made clear. The needs of mothers hardened into timelessly frozen properties of maternity as exem-plified in the housewife-mother figure, while the existence of the woman in paid work who was also a mother was inadmissible.[29]

Notions of 'apathy', a new inter-war vice catalogued by British sociological observers, also charted a course from the generally 'social' to the specifically reproductive. Its ravages were tracked across the new municipal housing estates, and in the electoral and childbearing shortcomings of the working class noted by amateur and professional sociologists. Apathy was the refusal to properly inhabit or to *be* the social. By the 1940s it had narrowed to the alleged 'defeatism' of the working-class couple who showed little eagerness to have the demographically desirable and socially responsible number of children. In such ways the shapeless ter-ritories of 'the social' expected allegiance from its inhabitants, although it was a homeland they had never chosen. In the British social-democratic and Fabian diction, its variant, 'the commun-ity', was by the time of the Second World War firmly established as an ideal site of civic responsibility, of rational maternity, of full waged labour, and hence of a promise of sensible familialism. Its threat was the 'problem family' studied in the 1930s; the experiment of Asterdorp, the ghetto for the rehabilitation of 'delinquent' families outside Amsterdam, attracted the keen interest of some British observers. The concerns of the 'social question' of the mid nineteenth century, the question of misery and poverty, had been more tightly specified: its gaze on the family as a site of social pathology fell on a woman; a mother who was the secret of its public failure. As Alva Myrdal wrote tersely in her *Nation and Family*, a social-democratic address to demographic issues: 'The female sex is a social problem.'[30]

*   *   *

Inter-war sociologies overshadowed and influenced a feminism which was noticeably torn between asserting the identity of 'women' in insisting on their differences from men, and an egalitarian emphasis, which defused difference to seek parity. The term 'feminism' itself, immediately after the First World War, and the granting of the partial women's suffrage, came to denote a narrowness, an anti-democratic or frankly bourgeois cast of mind, and an ungenerous rehearsal of old grievances which should have been decently laid to rest. Most damagingly, it came to be seen as a selfish antithesis to 'the social'. Certainly egalitarian and Fabian feminism exerted itself to demonstrate that on the contrary, the good of the social was its dearest concern. Nevertheless, these attempts to associate the emancipation of sex with the achievement of the ideal of citizenship and the democratised community were largely doomed. All feminisms were tarred with the same brush: they were an individualism-for-a-sex, and as such at odds with the advancement of the social whole. 'Sex-consciousness' and 'sex-antagonism' were deeply pejorative terms in 1918, and became so again in a second wave of revulsion in 1945 at the threatened resurrection of feminism. To look for comradeship between the sexes at the end of both wars seemed to be more honourable, and lively, than to nurse the corpse of old sexual battles; the vote had after all been won, and there were channels for discussing grievances. Feminism found itself in disgrace, while the franchise did not succeed in ushering in the finished democracy of the sexes, or even an amiable pulsation of different interests.

The strains for feminism in constantly addressing 'women' are most intense when there has been some transition, but an unfinished one: when 'humanity' stays obstinately impermeable, despite its ostensible democratisation. When disaffected women voters issue organised complaints, they may well be reproached precisely for their obduracy in remaining 'women'. So in Britain after 1918 and after 1928 when the universal franchise was obtained, and again after 1939, similar cries were heard; hadn't enfranchisement done away with the need for women to dwell so tediously upon their sex? The militant suffrage campaigns had also produced some revulsion among even the most sympathetic observers; the reiteration of 'women, women', became unbearable. The liberal heroine of May Sinclair's *The Tree of Heaven*, published in 1917, longed for the vote – but she could not endure the mass meetings:

For Dorothy was afraid of the Feminist Vortex, as her brother Michael had been afraid of the little vortex of school. She was afraid of the herded women. She disliked the excited faces, and the high voices skirling their battle cries, and the silly business of committees, and the platform slang. She was sick and shy before the tremor and the surge of collective soul, the swaying and heaving and rushing forward of the many as one. She would not be carried away by it; she would keep the clearness and hardness of her soul.[31]

Such an antipathy towards mass emotion, one of the many legacies of the First World War, could be devastating for the standing of militant feminism, especially where this was identified with a backward 'sexual antagonism'.

There was a consensus in the inter-war years that the older generation of feminists bored and irritated younger women. For it could not, it seemed, acknowledge the depths of men's sufferings, have the grace to fall silent on 'women', and instead espouse humanism. The First World War, that Calvary of men, was a sacrifice so vast that to press a nagging 'sex-consciousness' was shaming. The hero of Richard Aldington's *Death of a Hero* reflected whether 'the war had induced in me a peculiar resentment against women'.[32] The spectacle of 'women' still demanding rights could be seen as cheaply partisan failures of generosity. As Virginia Woolf characterised it in *Three Guineas*, 'feminism' had become irretrievably tarnished and redundant:

What more fitting than to destroy an old word, a vicious and corrupt word that has done much harm in its day and is now obsolete? The word 'feminist' is the word indicated. That word, according to the dictionary, means 'one who champions the rights of women'. Since the only right, the right to earn a living, has been won, the word no longer has a meaning. And a word without a meaning is a dead word, a corrupt word. . . . The word 'feminist' is destroyed: the air is cleared; and in that clearer air what do we see? Men and women working together for the same cause.[33]

And this, she continued, was really what the nineteenth-century feminisms had also been about:

'Our claim was no claim for women's rights only'; – it is Josephine Butler who speaks – 'it was larger and deeper; it was a claim for the rights of all – all men and women – to the respect in their persons that of the great principles of Justice and Equality and Liberty.'[34]

But an egalitarian feminism hung on to that name. The many small groups which were united under the National Union of Societies for Equal Citizenship, as well as more prominent campaigning organisations like the the Six Point Group, continued to press for legal, employment, and educational parity. In 1924, Winifred Holtby drew a distinction between these 'old feminists' and the 'new' variety. The latter stressed not equality, but the 'women's point of view':

Personally, I am a feminist, and an Old Feminist, because I dislike everything that feminism implies. I desire an end of the whole business, the demands for equality, the suggestions of sex warfare, the very name of feminist. I want to be about the work in which my real interests lie, the study of inter-race relationships, the writing of novels, and so forth. But while the inequality exists, while injustice is done and opportunity denied to the great majority of women, I shall have to be a feminist, and an Old Feminist, with the motto Equality First.[35]

In a similar spirit, the Six Point Group published a pamphlet in 1927 with the defensive title of 'Why Feminism Lives'. In it, Vera

Brittain put its endurance down to 'the incompleteness of the English franchise [which] represents but one symbol among many others of the incomplete recognition of women as human beings'.[36] For they still remained 'vaguely sub-human'; and it was this that drove on the seemingly anachronistic feminist, even against her inclinations:

> The fight for acknowledgement now bores rather than enthralls her; its postponement seems illogical, an anachronism, a waste of precious time. Her goal is the work of citizenship which awaits her as soon as she is allowed to play her full part in the making of civilisation; she continues to agitate, often a little wearily, only because she desires to abolish the need for agitation.[37]

To substitute the apparently more ethical longing to join humanity for sex-glorification – a vice comparable with class-glorification – was, however, a frustrating task. For, Vera Brittain explained,

> humanity is not a concrete, attainable qualification; it is an abstract idea. As such it is hard to transform into a slogan, and it has an academic flavour that renders it anathema to the present day youngest women, with their horror of anything that sounds heavy or 'pious', and their self-conscious individualism which regards self-scrificing devotion to any cause as 'pre-war' or 'démodé'.[38]

The impasse for feminism was acute in the 1920s and 1930s. It could not just repeat the charges issued by the 'old feminism'; nor could it simply discuss the position of women as class members with 'special needs'. The result was a nervous hesitation between 'equality' and 'difference', or a search for the fragile median position which saw women as 'different but equal'. Women's labour organisations, some of whose members were antipathetic to the very name of feminism, pressed for better maternity care and obstetric provision. Long campaigns for family allowances, the 'endowment of motherhood', were vigorously pursued by the Women's Co-operative Guild; through the 1920s there was, within the Labour Party, a frequently frustrated struggle to make contraceptive knowledge available to all. But the assertions of the needs of women in the family were liable to be captured by arguments about the natural propensities of women as mothers. Anyone might single out 'women' to pronounce upon. With alarm, Winifred Holtby quoted Oswald Mosley in his *The Greater Britain*. One of the longings of the British Union of Fascists, he had said, was for 'men who are men, and women who are women'.[39] By 1934 things had become all too clear in Europe. Winifred Holtby commented:

> Today, whenever women hear political leaders call their sex important, they grow suspicious. In the importance of the sex too often has laid the unimportance of the citizen, the worker and the human being.[40]

The social-democratic citizen, urged in the Fabian literature of the late 1930s to sharpen her civic consciousness by pursuing her reproductive and maternal duty to the community, was hardly an enticing figure. On the other hand, the woman worker, as the course of the Second World War made plain, was understood to be either girlish or nothing. A general solidarity of 'women' was an impossibility, given the common revulsion towards 'sex-glorification' and given class differences. Indeed, a curious litera-ture of women lamenting the loss of women domestic servants had appeared at the end of the First World War. Writings on the servant problem were devoted to the niceties of recruiting girls, of rearranging the house so that the awkwardness of humping the coals would be eased; or if the worst should come to the worst, of adjusting to daily service instead of having live-in help; titles like *The Labour Saving House*[41] abounded. Class divisions continued to ring through that socialist feminism of the 1920s and 1930s which, in order to combine work and maternity, relied on the background presences of the nurse, the maid, and the housekeeper. The writings of Naomi Mitchison and Dora Russell embodied this in their spirited demands that love and socialism should accompany each other, that 'new' feminists should be able to have both children and other occupations than the domestic.[42]

Theirs was a practical solution available to few, as they knew. At the level of theory, sexual difference remained an intractable conundrum. The famous 'five hundred pounds' and 'a room of one's own' was proposed by Virginia Woolf in 1928 to win a solid basis for intellectual liberation. Women's economic independence – even the independence of some – would, she held, allow the incandescent and unimpeded mind to leap onward, since all the grievances, preachings, and longings for revenge would have been 'fired out' of it. Nevertheless, she expressed a somewhat inconsistent longing for that life and colour which, she believed, 'differences' could bestow:

> It would be a thousand pities if women wrote like men, or lived like men, or looked like men, for if two sexes are quite inadequate, considering the vastness and variety of the world, how should we manage with one only? Ought not education to bring out and fortify the differences rather than the similarities? For we have too much likeness as it is.[43]

And yet the hateful 'sex-antagonism' could not afford a route for the development of a desirably sexed style. Contemplating an imaginary woman novelist, Virginia Woolf described her as having achieved such a style by careful evasion of any systematic and prior concentration on her gender:

> She wrote as a woman, so that her pages were full of that curious sexual quality which comes only when sex is unconscious of itself.[44]

But any 'sex-consciousness' would destroy this fluidity utterly, for it would falsely bifurcate the mind:

> And if it be true that it is one of the tokens of the fully developed mind that it does not think specially or separately of sex, how much harder it is to attain that condition now than ever before . . . No age can ever have been as stridently sex-conscious as our own; those innumerable books by men about women in the British Museum are a proof of it.[45]

Contemplating the 'sense of unmitigated masculinity' which she could see growing in Rome, hand in glove with nationalism, she conceived this too as a proof of the same weary vice: 'All who have brought about a state of sex-consciousness are to blame . . . All seducers and reformers are responsible.'[46] This is why it was 'fatal for anyone who writes to think of their sex', and why

It is fatal for a woman to lay the least stress on any grievance; to plead even with justice any cause; in any way to speak consciously as a woman.[47]

For the world could not, in truth, be divided into sexual camps. Women must face the fact that 'we go alone and that our relation is to the world of reality and not only to the world of men and women'.[48]

Her thinking is vividly torn. Both here in A Room of One's Own, and in Three Guineas, published a decade later, she was fully aware of social injustice founded on sexual divisions. Yet sex-consciousness was an impediment to change, she maintained; it clamped down the wrong limits, it distorted. Could there perhaps be some better feminist thinking which bypassed the partiality, the aggrieved tones, the taking of 'sides' against which she had inveighed in both books? In A Room of One's Own she mused about the Coleridgean androgynous mind, but without seizing upon the conception; 'Why do I feel that there are severances and oppositions in the mind, as there are strains from obvious causes in the body?'[49]

Here was another expression of the dilemma of modern feminism again; the impossibility of moving out from the recuperable reiterations of 'women' to the fullness of an unsexed humanity, without either getting stuck in the collectivity, or bypassing it completely. Feminism between the world wars was in a thoroughly uneasy state, its very name uncertain at best and any philosophical basis seemingly impossible to formulate and sustain. In the 1940s Simone de Beauvoir described the route for women's emancipation as 'moving from immanence to transcendence'.[50] Here she echoed Hegel on the need to move out of immersion in the details of the private life for the attainment of a true consciousness of self in the world. Yet how could this passage be ever made, if women were by definition the not-(yet)-human? And how could feminism, which spoke 'women', be the lever for this transition? The fact that 'women' and 'the social' had been so thoroughly folded into each other and rolled up together, had produced impossible consequences for modern feminism as a political philosophy. It could not but be incoherent, uncertain of what best to do with this unwieldy inheritance. To embrace and use it, to agitate for better social conditions for working-class women had tremendous tactical strengths, could forge useful alliances, and did produce real gains. Yet given that the very word 'women' was imbued in all political languages with domesticity in a broad sense, with a limiting notion of sociality – then this 'women' was also horribly circumscribed. That a heavy emphasis on the gender could be vulnerable to the most reactionary capture was made appallingly clear during the 1930s in Italy and in Germany. Meanwhile the irritations so strikingly repeated in the 1920s and 1930s – the vexations of women and men with feminism for representing the unimaginative spirit of an anti-democratic and redundant sex-consciousness – meant that 'women' could seem a dubious rallying-point even for progressive use.

To some degree, the difficulties were diluted in practice, in that 'feminism' as a term kept its older associations with well-off and often childless women, while labour and working women's organ-isations could be seen to deal with the 'real needs' of mothers and children. Yet this was an unsatisfactory compromise, incapable of steering through the deep uncertainties posed by the collective 'women' for feminism. For 'women' could not reside truthfully and contentedly within their differences as a sealed sociological group; but nor could they escape them to meld into humanity. If, to adapt Mary Wollstonecraft, the social should not overwhelm the human character,[51] then neither, to paraphrase Madame de Staël, could women succeed in leaving the ranks of nature to join the order of society. For if woman's entanglement in Nature had held her apart from Humanity, so did her newer entanglement in 'the social', since the latter was constructed so as to dislocate the political.[52] This second form of apartheid in the feminised 'social', however, was never more finished and absolute than the first assignation to the 'natural' had been. By no means did the allegedly natural dispositions of 'women' go into retreat once they emerged in the nineteenth century as sociological subjects. On the contrary, the 'natural' and the 'social' woman, now reinterpreted as willing inhabitants of the separate sphere, could vie with each other to make entry to the generally human fraught with further difficulty. The crucible here was the long battle for the suffrage.

4

The Womanly Vote

Fellow Countrywomen –
We call upon you to join us and help our fathers,
husbands and brothers, to free themselves and us from
political, physical and mental bondage . . .
We have been told that the province of woman is her
home, and that the field of politics should be left to
men; this we deny . . .

> (Address of the Female Political Union of Newcastle
> to their Fellow Countrywomen,
> *Northern Star*, 2 February 1839)

Woman runs a zigzag path between the feminine and
the human.

> (Lou Andreas-Salomé, 1899)

The history of women's suffrage gives rise to the less than celebratory reflection that categories often achieve their desired ends by
subdued routes – not gloriously and triumphantly, as if at the end
of an exhaustive, rewarded struggle to speak themselves, but
almost as by-products in the interstices of other discourses. The
initial demand for representation may be raised, too, in some
newly articulated gap between Humanity and Man, as the women
Republicans raised it in France; or in the less starkly delineated
gulfs between propertied voteless women and propertied voting
men which set the course of the nineteenth-century agitations in
Britain. The advancement of 'women' must always take its tone
from the differing backgrounds out of which their candidacy is to
be prised; it is never possible for 'women' to be amassed as
completely unshadowed subjects.

Nineteenth-century women, supposedly embodying the
benevolent truth of the social, could only present themselves as
potential electors by breaking out of the old massifications, and
departing, for instance, from the radical 'associationism' of the
1830s which had sought universal manhood suffrage. At such
moments the suffrage claim takes on the look of being the narrow
advocacy of a group interest, an individualism-for-a-sex. It must

insist on attention to 'women', and yet challenge what it takes to be inappropriate insistences on 'women' which spring from sexual conservatism. Here it shares the problem which vexes contemporary feminism. The latter, in undercutting bad usages of 'women', may nevertheless behave as if there is a true and apt level of feminisation to which it, feminism, has unique access by virtue of its scrupulous commitment to women and their needs. It claims the authority to speak for 'women's experience', and it may take this category to be self-evidently true and originary. But how, then, are the gulfs between the actual and the attributed conditions of 'women' to be characterised; how can feminist analysis, in speaking for what it holds to be the real, keep clear of the disfigurements of the rest of the world's opinions?

If the perennial impasse is put in this manner, it's insoluble. The winding course of later nineteenth and twentieth-century British feminisms is strewn with its skirmishes with what we could call over-feminisation, as well as under-feminisation. For often, feminists have had to speak in the same breath in and out of the category of 'women', with exhausting results. The drive towards political representation exposes the fluctuations of 'women', philosophically as well as strategically. So the first great obstacle of a question, How can women ever ascend into personhood and become voting citizens too, given their systematic exclusion from 'humanity'? is followed by successive problems: How, once enfranchised, can women make claims for their 'special needs' without losing the ground of generality that they have gained? As always, 'women' are illuminated in certain lights in advance; are already in some alliance with other political and philosophical languages which colour them. That is, feminism never has the option of putting forward its own uncontaminated, self-generated understandings of 'women': its 'women' too, is always thoroughly implicated in the discursive world.

This is particularly clear in the histories of suffrage campaigns, which must speak out for the rights of 'women', while the associations of 'women' alone debar them from being seriously received by legislators. At the same time, a peculiar transience is in play, for when 'women' are named by their protagonists as those who are excluded, this platform must aim at its own dissolution – the melting-back of women into the order of humanity by means of the franchise. Yet 'women' by definition cannot become 'citizens', cannot leave the baggage of their sex behind. So aspirants to the vote must during certain phases of their campaigns turn against the category of women, challenge its orthodox attributes in rewriting and minimising its ostensible significance, because it endlessly pins them down outside the general 'humanity' they must penetrate. Now 'women' becomes the standard of a restrictive association, and 'citizenship' is a glory to which women must aim, as in Olympe de Gouges' 1791 *Declaration of the Rights of Woman*. Then later, even centuries later, once the elusive citizenship has been nominally won through the suffrage, it appears instead as an artificially neutral limbo out of which the once-abandoned specificity of women must re-emerge to seek its own needs in the name of mothers, of women workers, or of another overlooked grouping. Post-suffrage feminisms continue the spasmodic oscillations between 'equality' and 'difference(s)' as they must; they cannot but echo and multiply the radical uncertainties of 'women' as it inches towards 'humanity' but never decisively arrives there.

*   *   *

Earlier attempts to propose women's candidacy for political rights foundered. One submission for the original draft of the Chartist petition in 1838 had included women in its plea for the extension of the franchise, under the shelter of universal suffrage. But their inclusion could not be covert enough so as to spare embarrassment to the cause; the risk that it might reduce the plausibility of universal manhood suffrage. It was abandoned. Disgrace enveloped French Republican women's battles to secure representation in the early 1790s. Olympe de Gouges, before she met her desolate end, had based her plea for rights on the equality of women's virtue; the efforts of those who, from different positions, had argued for the special social-surveillance capacities of Republican women, were also confounded.[1] Then whatever made the fight for the vote finally able to be waged consistently over a long period? Why did nineteenth-century suffragism escape those earlier truncations and eclipses?

Perhaps an answer lies in the increasing societal busyness of women and their slow legal advances – so that to some degree, the monotonous grand identity of 'woman' was being *de facto* scattered; that as more possibilities of enunciating 'women' came into life, the sexualised whole took on an anachronistic ring, just enough to allow women to be postulated as potential citizens. But this is, I think, an over-optimistic answer. The multiplications of 'women' carry fresh difficulties as well as advantages: the putative essence is constantly in tension with the local appearances, and swamps them from time to time. The collectivity, 'women', appears in newly broken forms in the nineteenth century; but none the less essence and appearance continue to fight for supremacy throughout.

If we look closely at some of the Parliamentary debates on British suffrage, we can see how the category of 'women' was dismembered on all sides. It was not possible to proclaim their goodness and their fitness as candidates in any unassailable manner. Not only because *not all* women were being advanced as voters by the proponents of the limited women's suffrage (for them, the franchise was to be extended to women with the same kinds of property-owning and other restrictions which hedged in the male electorate). But also because 'women' were thoroughly ensnared in an elaborate set of assumptions already in place; any political deployment of 'women' had no choice but to build upon, or try to undermine, this inherited foundation. It could never voice 'women' afresh. This limit was the lot of suffragist feminism.

The later nineteenth century's formal arguments twisted around a few great supporting poles. These were concerned with the 'natures', the 'interests', and the 'spheres' of women. It is true that the allocation of women to separate spheres was nothing new. The properly patriarchal theories of the seventeenth century mirrored the king's relation to his subjects in the husband's to his wife; the political philosophy of John Locke depicted the public and civic world as masculine, against the familial-feminine. The nineteenth-century suffrage debates, however, saw peculiar refashionings of this old division. Of course, to know why the parliamentary enfranchisement of women was so laborious and hesitant, and what obscured the passage of so many Reform bills, full studies of the wider party-political background, changes in Liberal and labour opinion, and the effects of the 1914–18 war are essential. Nevertheless, a sense of the tenacious vulnerabilities and uses of 'women' by all sides is also hugely important for suffrage history.

The first pole, that of 'women's interests' – the belief that women are distinct from men in what they want, that they would therefore vote as a class or mass, and that sex hostility would thus be formalised – had a power which became, if anything, more entrenched by the end of the nineteenth century. An early anonymous publication, *Women's Rights and Duties* of 1840, was confident that

> women have no political interests apart from men. The public measures that are taken, the restrictions or taxes imposed on the community, do not affect them more than male subjects. In all such respects the interests of the two sexes are identical. As citizens, therefore, they are sufficiently represented already. To give them the franchise would just double the number of voters, without introducing any new interest; and, far from improving society, few things would tend more to dissever and corrupt it.[2]

Then at once the companion assertion followed – that if women *did* have special interests in the shape of grievances to be redressed, these could not anyway be remedied by the vote:

> Interests of that description, being exclusively female, would come into collision, not, as in the other cases, with the interests of a class or party, but with those of the whole male sex, and one of two things would happen. Either one sex would be arrayed against one another in a sort of general hostility, or they would be divided amongst themselves. Than the first, nothing could possibly be devised more disastrous to the condition of women. They would be utterly crushed; the old prejudices would be revived against their education, or their meddling with household duties. Every man of mature age would probably stipulate, on marrying, that his wife should forswear the use of the franchise, and all ideas connected with political influence, or the coarse and degrading contentions of the elections.[3]

The writer hinted at the risk that unprincipled politicians might try to secure 'female parties' to support them over sex-specific issues, and might succeed in winning the allegiance, by manipulation, of 'the worst part of the sex'. More dangerous still, if women wanted to vote in a manner 'which was opposed to the interests or prejudices of their male relations', intimidation or bribery inflicted by their male kin might only intensify their 'timidity and comparative poverty'. This swaying between apprehensions of an institutionalised sex antagonism which might flow from the female franchise, and a domestic sex antagonism which might set husband to bullying wife, marked an enormous amount of subsequent debate. Most stress fell on the former fear. Certainly it was not confined to the camp of formal conservatism – and indeed liberal anti-suffragists could always argue that the Tory party would find itself enriched by a new natural constituency of propertied women voters. The Liberal, Captain Maxse, addressed the Electoral Reform Conference in 1874 thus:

> I hold it to be the duty of men to protect women, and to represent their interests in Parliament. We shall commit a fatal error if we set women up in political hostility to men.[4]

The continuing assumption was that 'women' would form a united body, and would vote according to a sex-specific point of view – as if, on all questions, there must always be such a thing. This assumption was rarely directly challenged by pro-suffragists: not surprising, given their need to emphasise 'women'. To fight for the rights and visibility of a group was hardly likely to make the tactic of deconstructing its mass a pressing one. The suffrage lecturer, Arabella Shore, restricted her defence against the charge of sexual antagonism to pointing out that women sought only to elect male representatives for themselves:

> As to the charge of hostility, it amazes me. We ask that we may help in the choice of men to maintain a masculine Government. We are not demanding the vote that we may elect women instead of, and in opposition to men.[5]

But such an answer could hardly defuse the sex-war charge. The conservative Beresford Hope, in an 1871 House of Commons debate, emphasised that 'the womanly nature' already exerted enough indirect influence on family men who voted – it 'had quite as much play in making up the national mind as could healthily be desired'.[6] But, he held, if women were enfranchised, a sex-linked distortion of the electorate would come into being. Once women, naturally allied to the social sphere, wielded power, a disproportionate narrowness would ensue:

> The character of the legislation of a woman-chosen Parliament would be the increased importance which would be given to questions of a quasi social or philanthropic character (viewed with regard to the supposed interests, or the partisan bias of

special classes, rather than to broader considerations of the public weal) in excess of the great constitutional and international issues which the legislature was empanelled to try.[7]

A more dignified and congratulatory conviction of women's distinctive philanthropic mission allowed the female signatories to the 1889 *An Appeal Against Female Suffrage* to write:

It is because we are keenly alive to the enormous value of their special contribution to the community, that we oppose what seems to us likely to endanger that contribution. We are convinced that the pursuit of a mere outward equality with men is for women not only vain but demoralising. It leads to a total misconception of woman's true dignity and special mission. It tends to personal struggle and rivalry, where the only effort of both the great divisions of the human family should be to contribute the characteristic labour and the best gifts of each to the common stock.[8]

These signatories were, as contemporary pro-suffragists tartly pointed out, by and large the wives of great men rather than women of great distinction in their own right. Although they included the then Miss Beatrice Potter, she was outflanked by Mrs T. H. Green, Mrs Leslie Stephen, Mrs Huxley, Mrs Henry Hobhouse, Mrs Matthew Arnold and Mrs Arnold Toynbee. Their *Appeal* summarised the 'considered' anti-suffragism of many years. It repeated the old assertion that in so far as women possessed special interests, those could be catered for by the present arrangements:

all the principal injustices of the law towards women have been amended by means of the existing constitutional machinery; and with regard to those that remain, we see no signs of any unwillingness on the part of Parliament to deal with them. On the contrary, we remark a growing sensitiveness to the claims of women, and the rise of a new spirit of justice and sympathy among men, answering to those advances made by women in education, and the best kind of social influence, which we have already noticed and welcomed.[9]

They rehearsed the fear of a clash of sex against sex in terms almost identical to those of fifty years and more before:

With regard to the business or trade interests of women, – here, again, we think it safer and wiser to trust to organisation and self-help on their own part, and to the growth of a better public opinion among the men workers, than to the exercise of a political right which may easily bring women into direct and hasty conflict with men.[10]

And, insisted the women anti-suffragists, again echoing a venerable defence, women themselves did not want the franchise:

the mass of those immediately concerned in it are notoriously indifferent; there has been no serious and general demand for it, as is always the case if a grievance is real and reform necessary.[11]

Gladstone in 1892 argued the same point in his letter to Samuel Smith:

There has never within my knowledge been a case in which the franchise has been extended to a large body of persons generally indifferent about receiving it. But here, in addition to a widespread indifference, there is on the part of large numbers of women who have considered the matter for themselves, the most positive objection and strong disapprobation.[12]

Yet this common objection, that the suffrage was over the heads of and irrelevant if not decidedly unwelcome to most women, was never much amplified. In the same way that the pro-suffragists could hardly embark on a tactical deconstruction of 'women', the antis had their reasons for leaving the sanctity of 'women' *en bloc*, by and large, alone. This was not, I suspect, merely due to the embarrassing fact of the waves of working-class pro-suffrage activity, which put paid to the claim that all agitators were 'ladies' alone. It must also have been determined by the salience of 'women's interests' and their distinctive social role for the anti-suffrage case. If 'women' were to be taken apart and that wholeness weakened by the claims of factions among them, much would have crumbled, too much to be palatable to anti-suffragism.

John Stuart Mill, arguing unsuccessfully for electoral reform in the House of Commons in 1867, proposed a sophisticated retort to the old charge:

We are told, Sir, that women do not wish for the suffrage. If the fact were so, it would only prove that all women are still under this deadening influence; that the opiate still benumbs their mind and conscience. But great numbers of women do desire the suffrage, and have asked for it by petitions to this House. How do we know how many more thousands there may be who have not asked for what they do not hope to get; or for fear of what may be thought of them by men, or by other women; or from the feeling, so sedulously cultivated in them by their education – aversion to make themselves conspicuous?[13]

Still, he ventured, even if women's induced reticence was allowed, and the vote bestowed, those who didn't want it, wouldn't use it:

either they will not register, or if they do, they will vote – as their male relatives advise – by which, as the advantage will probably be about equally shared among all classes, no harm will be done.[14]

In short, it need not be assumed that women would exert a block vote, behave in concert, or be bullied by unwilling possession of the franchise into deploying it. So, for Mill, the unification of 'the woman's vote' could be dismembered. At the same time, he proposed that enfranchising women who might well behave dissimilarly, would nevertheless ennoble the category of women as an abstraction:

Meanwhile an unworthy stigma would be removed from the whole sex. The law would cease to declare them incapable of serious things; would cease to proclaim that their opinions and wishes are unworthy of regard, on things which concern them equally with men, and on many things which concern them much more than men . . . If only one woman in 20,000 used the suffrage, to be declared capable of it would be a boon to all women. Even that theoretical enfranchisement would remove a weight from the expansion of their facilities, the real mischief of which is much greater than the apparent.[15]

But here 'women' return as a mass whose emancipation would make them collectively less narrowed, hemmed-in and trivialised; once the 'stigma' of lightheadedness was removed, a true elevation of all would follow. Here the totality of sex was re-admitted to the argument *for* the suffrage cause, while before it had been challenged to weaken the anti-suffragist case. Tactics had to be elastic, as were philosophies, in the face of the obdurate apartness of 'women' which determined the whole debate.

*   *   *

Another great pole of argument – from women's 'natures' and the degree of their distinctiveness – illustrates the same systematic contortions which beset the notion of their 'interests.' That women were ineradicably *sui generis* and hence not plausible members of an electorate was a devastatingly tenacious supposition. In 1843 Mrs Hugo Reid set out a circumspect challenge to it:

> We do not mean to assert that man and woman are strictly the same in their nature, or the character of their minds; but simply, that in the grand characteristics of their nature they are the same, and that where they differ, it is in the minor features; that they resemble far more than they differ from each other.[16]

Yet half a century later, Gladstone echoed the enduring conviction that, being divinely bestowed, distinctions of sex were radical and insurmountable:

> A permanent and vast difference of type has been impressed upon women and men respectively by the Maker of both . . . I for one am not prepared to say which of the two sexes has the higher and which has the lower province. But I recognize the subtle and profound character of the differences between them, and I must again, and again, and again, deliberate before aiding in the issue of what seems like an invitation by public authority to the one to renounce as far as possible its own office, in order to assume that of the other.[17]

If minimising sexual difference was, in the teeth of this well-entrenched theorem, a doomed strategy for pro-suffragists, then there was another tack to try, which many attempted – to admit difference, but render it irrelevant to the argument. The social reformer, Frances Power Cobbe, in her 1868 article, 'Criminals, idiots, women, minors, is the classification sound?', pointed out that 'equality' had not, historically, been the ground for bestowing civil liberty anyway; and

Even for political rights, among all the arguments eagerly cited last year against extending the franchise, no one though it worth while to urge that the class proposed to be admitted to them was, or was not, physically, intellectually, or morally inferior to the classes which already possessed it. As for civil rights – the right to hold property, to make contracts, to sue and be sued – no class, however humble, stupid, and even vicious, has even been denied them since serfdom and slavery came to an end . . . [We reply:] Granted let me be physically, intellectually and morally your inferior. So long as you allow I possess moral responsibility and sufficient intelligence to know right from wrong (a point I conclude you will concede, else why hang me for murder?) I am quite content. It is *only* as a moral and intelligent being I claim my civil rights.[18]

But, of course, the vigour which informed believers in specifically sexual differences was easily proof against such sophisticated political philosophy. Their arguments could not be side-stepped thus, and few suffragists emulated Frances Power Cobbe's defence. Instead they tried to invert difference, to make a positive value out of it. So in 1877 Arabella Shore responded to the well-worn charges of women's innate peculiarities:

Granting the favourite charge that she is more emotional and impulsive than man, what then? Can the more or less of qualities common to the race make the one half of a nation fit to be represented, the other not? Is the Irishman disqualified for a vote because he is more impulsive than the Englishman? And may not this variety in the proportion of qualities be an advantage rather than otherwise? May there not be a danger from the exclusive preponderance of a certain set of tendencies, and may not the infusion of a new moral element sometimes strengthen the higher considerations which might be in danger of being postponed to merely commercial, or other self-regarding interests?[19]

Replying to Mrs Humphrey Ward's anti-suffrage appeal in *The Nineteenth Century*, Millicent Garrett Fawcett put this position in a yet more forceful manner. Difference itself *made* the case for the extension of the vote, so let it not be conjured away or subdued:

We do not want women to be bad imitations of men; we neither deny nor minimise the differences between men and women. The claim of women to representation depends to a large extent on those differences. Women bring something to the service of the state different from that which can be brought by men. Let this fact be frankly recognised and let due weight be given to it in the representative system of the country.[20]

The anti-suffragist *Appeal* had argued that women's 'special contribution to the community' could only be endangered by the limited franchise. Mrs Fawcett, a leader of the 'moderate' suffragists, and committed to the limited franchise, determined to stress the virtues of sexual difference in support of this circumscribed ambition. Much liberal suffragism by the end of the nineteenth century had pledged itself to the same emphasis – although it is difficult to know just how much this strategy was determined by real conviction.

Again this reliance on difference contrasts with the positions taken by Mill in his speech to the Commons in 1867. Here he insisted that women were becoming less markedly unlike men, and that this was a deeply desirable development for both sexes. The old apartheid, he believed, was withering away, a relic of the time when the sexes

were separate in their thoughts, because they were separate equally in their amusements and in their serious occupations . . . All this, among the educated classes, is now changed. The man no longer gives his spare hours to violent exercises and boisterous conviviality with male associates; the two sexes now pass their lives together; the women of a man's family are his habitual society; the wife is his chief associate, his most confidential friend, and often his trusted adviser.[21]

Given the strength and intimacy of this constant association, Mill continued, would not the institutionalised inferiority of the voteless wife drag down the husband? His is virtually an argument from a feared contamination:

Now, does a man wish to have for his companion so closely linked with him, one whose thoughts are alien to those which occupy his own mind – one who can neither be a help, a comfort, nor a support, to his own noblest feelings and pur-

poses? Is this close and almost exclusive companionship compatible with women's being warned off all large subjects – being
taught that they ought not to care for what it is men's duty to
care for, and that to have any serious interests outside the
household is stepping beyond their province? Is it good for man
to live in complete communion of thoughts and feelings with
one who is studiously kept inferior to himself, whose earthly
interests are forcibly confined to within four walls, and who
cultivates, as a grace of character, ignorance and indifference
about the most inspiring subjects, those among which his
highest duties are cast? Does anyone suppose that this can
happen without detriment to the man's own character? Sir, the
time is now come, when, unless women are raised to the level of
men, men will be pulled down to theirs.[22]

Mill's argument for the elevation of women within marriage is
made more intelligible if we set beside it those simple and pro-
grammatic assertions of an incorrigible sexual difference made by
anti-suffrage speakers in the Commons debate on the Women's
Disabilities Bill in 1871. Mr Beresford Hope declared:

If this Bill should pass, and the number of emancipated women
were found to produce no appreciable change in the quality of
the representation in the House, then he would say that they
had made a great disturbance to gain something very small
indeed; but, on the other hand, if it were found to cause any
serious alteration in the character of the representation, then,
with all due respect to all the new constituencies, he believed
that the alteration would be shown in the deterioration and not
in the improvement of the quality of Parliament. On this head
he desired to speak plainly. It was not a question of whether the
male or the female intellect was the superior one. He simply said
that they were different, and that the difference made man more
capable of direct government and women more fitted for private
influence. There were in the world women of a manlike mind – a
Mrs Somerville or a Miss Martineau – and there were now and
then men of feminine softness: but he reasoned from the generality and not from marked exceptions.[23]

Believing in absolute distinctions, this speaker foresaw a distinctive womanly vote which would enact the emotional peculiarities
of the new voters:

We should have more wars for an idea, or hasty alliances with scheming neighbours, more class cries, permissive legislation, domestic perplexities, and sentimental grievances. Our legislation would develop hysterical and spasmodic features, partaking more of the French and American system than reproducing the tradition of the English Parliament.[24]

Mrs Humphrey Ward's *An Appeal Against Female Suffrage* played more mildly upon the same theme. A volatile female emotionality would import hysteria into politics – by implication, a sanguine realm in its undisturbed masculinity:

The quickness to feel, the willingness to lay aside prudential considerations in a right cause, which are amongst the peculiar excellencies of women, are in their right place when they are used to influence the more highly trained and developed judgement of men. But if this quickness of feeling could be immediately and directly translated into public action, in matters of vast and complicated political import, the risks of politics would be enormously increased, and what is now a national blessing might easily become a national calamity.[25]

Women's influence took its blessedness precisely from its indirection, as if the male vote acted as a filter for its highly charged impurities:

On the one hand, then, we believe that to admit women to the ordinary machinery of political life would inflame the partisanship and increase the evils, already so conspicuous, of that life, would tend to blunt the special moral qualities of women, and so to lessen the national reserves of moral force; and, on the other hand, we dread the political and practical effects which, in our belief, would follow on such a transformation as is proposed, of an influence which is now beneficent largely because it is indirect and gradual.[26]

Proponents of women's suffrage decades earlier had attacked these theories of subliminal influence in vain. In her 1877 address to the London National Society for Women's Suffrage, Arabella Shore had denounced the great Nature-argument . . . First one would like to know when it is so glibly said that Nature is opposed to this or that, what is meant by Nature. Is it ancient usage or established convention, the law or custom of our country, training, social position, the speaker's own particular fancy or prejudice, or what? . . . It seems that for a woman to manage property, carry on large businesses, be a farmer, a merchant, a parish overseer, a clerk in various capacities, a municipal elector, or member of a School Board, or even a Sovereign, is not against Nature, but to give a vote for a Member of Parliament is . . . We feel that politics means legislation, and that legislation enters into questions in which we have a right and necessity to be interested. We cannot separate domestic politics from social conditions of life. If then we are told that we have nothing to do with politics, we can but answer that politics have a great deal to do with us.[27]

Yet the double-edged assumption of closeness between women and the social sphere was implacably resistant to being translated into electoral politics, so long as the central conviction endured that 'women' was a distinct natural species. Arabella Shore spoke directly against the supposed wholeness of 'man', and the ancillary being of 'woman':

The language of these theorists implies that man is, properly speaking, all human nature, with all his faculties perfectly balanced, and woman an imperfect anomalous accessory, a bundle of instincts always foolish, and mostly mischievous . . . Women vary as men vary, they are moulded and modified by the same diversified influences as affect men, birth, education, family-belongings, social atmosphere; and these variations apart, Englishwomen are of the same race as Englishmen, and partake of the same strong national character. So that, on the whole, Magna Carta is not likely to be repealed by the female descendents of those who won it for us.[28]

But one assault returned and returned to undermine any such pleas that 'women' were demonstrably not homogeneous. That was the argument from physiology. The 1889 *Appeal*'s women signatories fell back on it:

we believe that the emancipating process has now reached the limits fixed by the physical constitution of women, and by the fundamental difference which must always exist between their main occupations and those of men. The care of the sick and the insane; the treatment of the poor; the education of children; in all these matters, and others besides, they have made good their claim to larger and more extended powers. We rejoice in it.[29]

Physiological femininity underlay these 'social' preoccupations of women, while it forbade their crossing into the realm of politics, 'questions of foreign or colonial policy, or of grave constitutional change'[30] which demanded a different form of judgement. Women's social alliances and higher morality would, the signatories believed, justly admit them to local and indirect power:

we would give them their full share in the State of social effort and social mechanism: we look for their increasing activity in that higher State which rests on thought, conscience, and moral influence; but we protest against their admission to direct power in the State which does rest upon force – the State in its administrative, military, and financial aspects – where the physical capacity, the accumulated experience and inherited training of men ought to prevail without the harassing interference of those who, though they may be partners with men in debate, can in these matters never be partners with them in action.[31]

Useless to retort that the involvement of the majority of enfranchised men with the 'administrative, military, and financial aspects' of national life was hardly direct. The appeal to the disabling physiology of women derived at least some of its forcefulness from its proximity to the doctrine of separate spheres, a potent conflation of the demarcated interests, natures, and social alliances of women. This conflation only intensified in the course of the nineteenth-century suffrage debates. Harriet Taylor had dealt with it sharply in 1851:

Many persons think they have sufficiently justified the restrictions on women's field of action, when they have said that the pursuits from which women are excluded are *unfeminine* and that the *proper sphere* of women is not politics or publicity, but private and domestic life.

We deny the right of any portion of the species to decide for another portion, or an individual for another individual, what is and what is not their 'proper sphere'. The proper sphere for all human beings is the largest and highest which they are able to attain to. What this is, cannot be ascertained, without complete liberty of choice.[32]

But the yawning gap between 'women' and 'all human beings' continued to thwart this defiant liberalism.

* * *

The third great pole of anti-suffrage contention was that of the 'separate sphere' of women. This depended heavily on their putative closeness to the social: it reworked their separate 'interests' and 'differences' under the banner of the social to produce a forceful third item. The suffrage campaigner Barbara Bodichon was among those in the 1860s who tried another tactic: to build on this established association and edge it towards the political:

the mere fact of being called upon to enforce an opinion by a vote, would have an immediate effect in awakening a healthy sense of responsibility. There is no reason why these women should not take an active interest in all the social questions – education, public health, prison discipline, the poor laws, and the rest – which occupy Parliament, and by bringing women into hearty co-operation with men, we gain the benefit not only of their work, but of their intelligent sympathy.[33]

In similar vein, Mill tried to start an argument for the suffrage from an acknowledgement of domestic preoccupations, in order to push them outwards if not to erode them:

The ordinary occupations of most women are, and are likely to remain, principally domestic; but the notion that these occupations are incompatible with the keenest interest in national affairs, and in all the great interests of humanity, is as utterly futile as the apprehension, once sincerely entertained, that artisans would desert their workshops and their factories if they were taught to read.[34]

At the same time, this presumably political suggestion – Mill was speaking to the Commons – was both undercut and superficially confirmed by his optimism that the separation of spheres was, anyway, withering away within private lives:

> We talk of political revolutions, but we do not sufficiently attend to the fact that there has taken place around us a silent domestic revolution; women and men are, for the first time in history, really each other's companions.[35]

It followed, then, that enfranchising women would prevent the slide of their husbands into their lower world of gossip and trivia, 'personalities'. Mill was defeated; twenty years later, the *Westminster Review* proposed a rather Fabian argument, on communitarian not personal-ethical grounds. The vote should be bestowed willy-nilly for the benefit of 'the community':

> It is clear that if duly qualified women desire . . . to be enrolled as citizens, they are entitled to have their demands granted. But it is equally clear that, even if they do not desire it, the State is entitled to make them assume the responsibility of citizenship if it be proved that it is for the welfare of the State that they should be thus burdened. That doctrine is universally admitted in the case of men. Upon it rests the law of conscription . . . compulsory education and indeed of all taxation, and thus women are included in its scope . . . It is a loss to society that it should not have the benefit of women's ability reflected in Parliament, to aid in the discussion of the vast number of social subjects, all of which affect women as keenly as men.[36]

Even the most managerial advocacy of the suffrage, it seems, could not resist repeating the supposition of the close alliance between 'women' and 'the social', to be cemented by the vote. This alliance still could not reduce the extremity of the gulf between 'women' considered *en masse* and the political realm. Again, the 'wives of distinguished men' who signed the *Appeal Against Female Suffrage* of 1889 confirm how this gulf could serve opposing causes. For them, women's proximity to the social constituted an argument for *refusing* the step of the vote into the political. Local concerns were admirable:

> we are heartily in sympathy with all the recent efforts which have been made to give women a more important part of those

affairs of the community where their interests and those of men are equally concerned; where it is possible for them not only to decide but to help in carrying out, and where, therefore, judgment is weighted by a true responsibility, and can be guided by experience and the practical information which comes from it. As voters for or members of School Boards, Boards of Guardians, and other important public bodies, women have now opportunities for public usefulness which must promote the growth of character, and at the same time strengthen among them the social sense and habit.[37]

Thus far, but no further. Women citizens without the vote, they felt, made for a better order of things, in which the separation of natural spheres might be maintained for the general good. Let women make their own form of contribution:

For whatever may be the duty and privilege of the parliamentary vote for men, we hold that citizenship is not dependent upon or identical with the possession of the suffrage. Citizenship lies in the participation of each individual in effort for the good of the community. And we believe that women will be more valuable citizens, will contribute more to the national life without the vote than with it.[38]

The old notion of a species-specific temperamental volatility reappeared in this manifesto; perhaps Mrs Humphrey Ward felt that her own authorship escaped its implications.[39]

That women were already adequately represented by means of their subterranean workings on their male relatives' vote was the oldest plank of anti-suffragism. There was a 'family' principle of repesentation which was not to be disturbed. In 1892 Gladstone – who undoubtedly had less elevated motives as well for his stance – voiced his

fear lest beginning with the State, we should eventually be found to have intruded into what is yet more fundamental and more sacred, the precinct of the family, and should dislocate, or injuriously modify, the relations of domestic life.[40]

Twenty-five years earlier, Mill had objected that indirect power was not responsible power, and therefore in order to render it moral, it must be made direct. He did not choose to question the supposition that all women really did possess the fêted influence:

> Sir, it is true that women have great power. It is part of my case that they have great power; but they have it under the worst possible conditions, because it is indirect and therefore irresponsible. I want to make this great power a responsible power. I want to make the woman feel her conscience interested in its honest exercise. I want her to feel that it is not given to her as a mere means of personal ascendancy. I want to make her influence work by a manly interchange of opinion, and not only by cajolery. I want to awaken in her the political point of honour. Many a woman already influences greatly the political conduct of the men connected with her, and sometimes by force of will, actually governs it; but she is never supposed to have anything to do with it; the man whom she influences, and perhaps misleads, is alone responsible; her power is like the back-stairs influence of a favourite.[41]

Again, 'women' are characterised as embodiments of sentiment, as cloying courtiers whose moral elevation is imperative to prevent the mutual decline of both sexes. Indeed 'women' had better be masculinised, Mill pleads:

> men are afraid of manly women; but those who have considered the nature and power of social influence well know, that unless there are manly women, there will not much longer be manly men.[42]

Given the psychologisations of the female sex he had already deployed, this stratagem was the only means available to Mill, however incongruously it may have rung in the Commons. To shift his ground from arguing the mutual corruptions of 'indirect influence', he turned to a less highly charged ground of attack: the inadequacy of indirection:

> The operatives for instance; are they not virtually represented by the representations of their employers? Are not the interests of the employers and that of the employed, when properly understood, the same? To insinuate the contrary, is it not the horrible crime of setting class against class? . . . And what is

more, are not all employers good, kind, benevolent men, who
love their workpeople, and always desire to do what is most for
their good? All these assertions are as true, and as much to the
purpose, as the corresponding assertions respecting men and
women . . . Workmen need other protection than that of their
employers, and women other protection than that of their men. I
should like to have a Return laid before this House of the
number of women who are annually beaten to death, kicked to
death, or trampled to death by their male protectors.[43]

To enfranchise only some women would hardly be a radical step:

Sir, grievances of less magnitude than the law of the property of
married women, when suffered by parties less inured to passive
submission, have provoked revolutions. We ought not to take
advantage of the security we feel against any such consequence
in the present case, to withhold from a limited number of
women that moderate amount of participation in the enactment
and improvement of our laws, which this Motion solicits for
them, and which would enable the general feelings of women to
be heard in this House through a few male representatives.[44]

This was, he continued, a right enjoyed by 'every petty trade or
profession'. Mill's amendment, nevertheless, was lost by 73 to 196
votes; and as we have seen, anti-suffrage opinion throughout the
next few decades repeated the old grounds – of adequate and
indirect – or adequate, because indirect – influence.

*   *   *

A burning and practical dislike of the idea of female voters, one
which affected Liberal opinion profoundly, was rooted elsewhere.
Since the limited franchise, once extended, would have admitted
some women property-owners, their political conservatism was
feared. Here not so much 'women' trailing their affective attributes were repugnant, but the spectre of a fresh phalanx of Tory
voters. So some de-sexing of the heavily sexualised woman voter
did come about; but at a paralysing cost to the suffragists. Viewed
as prospective Tories, they were unenticing causes for much
Liberal opinion to espouse. Mill's principled liberalism was not
isolated; but to the end of the 1880s, a great weight of political
Liberal antagonism bore down on the extension of the limited

franchise. Captain Maxse's speech to the Electoral Reform Conference in 1874 encapsulated the radical and liberal apprehensions:
the natural psychological conservatism of 'women' would translate
itself directly into political allegiances, democracy would suffer
further injuries as a result, and the ignoble tentacles of the clergy
would have a means of reaching further into public life:

> It is said, however, that men have not represented the interests
> of women in the legislature. But if women have been badly
> represented in Parliament hitherto – so have men! The highest
> interests of neither have yet been represented in the legislature:
> we have all suffered alike from the selfish class rule. The object
> of our present movement is to represent all classes and the
> women in them . . . It is my opinion that the collective thought
> of women – that is, the opinion of the majority of women – will
> be adverse to enlightenment and progress. I must decline to
> regard the ladies who demand Woman Suffrage as the mental
> representatives of their sex.[45]

For unlike these admirable exceptions, most women occupied the
apathetic and domesticated feminine standpoint:

> They seem to be incapable of sympathizing with great causes –
> they have a strong predilection for personal Institutions. As a
> rule they are completely without interest in great national ques-
> tions. Theirs is essentially the private life point of view.[46]

Their petty conservatism, harnessed by the Clergy – 'their instinc-
tive submission to *whatever is* and their dread of ideas, which
have not the sanction of custom' – would, dignified by the franchise, result in a catastrophe for progress:

> The hands of the clock are to be put back that women may pass
> through men's accomplished experiences, and we are to be
> delivered over for a long period of uninterrupted Tory rule![47]

The slippage here between an attributed psychological conservatism and an expected political conservatism is complete, and is
well in excess of any realistic assessment of the voting behaviour
of women property-owners. Yet the radical attack on the limited
franchise took a further twist: the charge that it was not, in any

event, a true enfranchisement of all women, but merely of the propertied and single:

> The effect of embodying it in legislation will be that propertied widows and spinsters will possess the franchise not on account of their sex, but on account of their property, while marriage will stand out as a political disqualification. The ladies say that they take the franchise as they find it; but they are bound to recognise that the present electoral law was constructed solely with a view to male suffrage, and that it cannot be made, without some special wife qualification which they do not propose, to include woman suffrage.[48]

The 'class measure' of the limited suffrage was not even open, then, to the anyway dubious excuse that it represented sexual emancipation; only some women would become reincarnated as privileged agents of an 'additional means of class oppression'. How could such a bleak deconstruction of 'women' be countered? It was a harsh irony of debate in the 1870s that women were either excessively women, and disqualified by means of their presumed latent hysteria – or that when the limitations of the suffrage were considered, they were not women at all. Arabella Shore dismissed the accusation of 'stagnant Toryism' by pointing out that *how* a newly enfranchised person might vote was not the principled issue:

> if it be true that there are more Conservatives among women than men, this cannot to the true Liberal be a just reason for their exclusion. What business have we to make or maintain laws to exclude the political party whose views we dislike?[49]

Conceding to the forces of political expediency, she added that a monolithic sexed vote was not a real threat anyway:

> It would be more fair to say that in politics women ordinarily adopt the opinion of the men around them than that all women have but one opinion amongst them. If this leads generally to Toryism, we can only say that on Constitutional principles the party that has a majority in the nation has a right to a majority in the House.[50]

Although, she added circumspectly, enlightened female opinion
was thoroughly Liberal. Of such a persuasion were the suffragists,
experienced through philanthropic work on women's needs, and
'public and social questions'; they, and working women, were the
two main classes of contenders for the vote. It was untrue that only
the conservative élite sought the vote – and that out of self-
interest:

> For this is not a 'ladies' question, it is a 'women's' question, and
> I and many others know how the working order of women feel
> their practical grievances, and how they would hail any change
> that promised to amend them.[51]

Indeed, it became clear that several – though not all – working
women's organisations would energetically support the limited
suffrage. The new life which transformed and revived the suffrage
campaigns in the late 1890s and early 1900s included many socialist women in the growing labour movement. The new Independent Labour Party committed itself to the vote for women. The
Women's Co-operative Guild after 1889 campaigned, on the
whole, most vigorously for it, as did at least a part of the Women's
Trade Union League. Their conviction was that since the ideally
democratic solution of universal adult suffrage did not look, then,
like 'practical politics', at least the limited women's suffrage
would, by admitting women householders, act as the thin end of
the desired wedge. And it would allow those working women,
often widows and spinsters, who were householders some
immediate access to political influence.[52]

Still the familiar issue continued to torment much socialist and
liberal opinion. Adult suffrage was for many the more desirable
politics. The partial suffrage for women would bring about
immediate parity between some women and some men, but at the
cost of that undemocratic 'some'. The bulk of the Women's Trade
Union League, as well as the newer Women's Labour League,
dedicated their efforts towards adult suffrage, and most of the
labour leadership as well as its rank and file inclined, like most
Liberals, in the same direction. By 1907, Mrs Pankhurst's
Women's Social and Political Union had turned its hopes decisively away from these quarters, and towards the Conservative
Party; and had turned its tactics towards militance. At the same

time, the well-rehearsed dread of women's natural reaction, and its aptness to produce a swollen Tory vote, continued unabated.

The massive engagement of women in philanthropic work drew many of them towards suffragism in the 1890s; some of the most ardent campaigners, like Charlotte Despard and Emmeline Pethick-Lawrence, moved from welfare to politics. Nevertheless, philanthropy was an uncertain training-ground for Parliamentary agitation, since the 'social concern' of women might, as we have seen from earlier decades, be harnessed to the 'separate spheres' argument to confirm their remoteness from harder politics. Yet some did believe that the power of the vote was an essential lever for rapid reform. In his *Women and Philanthropy* Frank Prochaska points out that

> Lady Henry Somerset's powerful British Women's Temperance Association, for example, set up a political department and announced that votes for women were essential if there was to be temperance reform.[53]

But he emphasises that women's vast immersion in philanthropic efforts did not lead to any automatic flow of sympathy with The Cause, and that the engagement of those who did sympathise was rarely compulsive. They became suffrage society workers as well as moral reformers or institutional visitors, in much the same spirit. This was double-edged. Indeed, these types of benevolent women 'were also prominent among the anti-suffragists, and their charitable role was in tune with the anti-suffrage view of the world'.[54] Those of whichever sex who viewed the phenomenon of women philanthropists at the turn of the century through anti-suffrage lenses feared that such women, once enfranchised and schooled to a latent 'political emotionalism', would drift into a 'sentimental socialism' and vote accordingly.

While the impact of female philanthropic involvement was ambiguous, the old arguments of the 1860s still raged on. The conviction of women's temperamental and intellectual apartness continued to militate against their enfranchisement to a surprisingly late date. Martin Pugh quotes Asquith's vehement anti-feminism in 1920; to him, women electors were 'hopelessly ignorant of politics, credulous to the last degree and flickering with gusts of sentiment like candles in the wind'.[55] In his study of

anti-suffragism, *Separate Spheres*, Brian Harrison quotes
Asquith's belief that sexual differences were indelible bequests of
Nature, and so proof against any attempts at levelling. However
much political expediency may have reinforced this particular
apostle of difference, it remains true that a felt weight continued to
be placed by anti-suffragists on the supposed physiological
unfitness of women. This half-hidden objection was based on
menstruation, while the overt complaint was of the declining
birthrate, hysteria, invalidism, pregnancies of women; their num-
erical dominance which would make it undemocratic to enfranchise every one of them; their ineptness at contributing to the
governing of the Empire and contending with the toughness of the
real political world; and their susceptibility to 'priestly influences'
which might entice them to obscurantist causes.[56]

To ascribe the continual frustrations of the limited suffrage
campaign only to the espousal of a nobler democracy – adult
suffrage – by liberal and labour tendencies would overlook the
powers of repeated older doubts shared by many across the
political spectrum. The conviction, common to some members of
all parties, that the female electorate would inevitably vote along
sexed lines persisted into the 1920s, as did the objection that if
women were enfranchised altogether, men would be unfairly
outnumbered. Overblown conceptions of how rigorously men
deliberated when they cast a vote continued in the supposition
that women, sunk in household matters, would lack the perspicac-
ity to make a properly nuanced choice of party. Some conservatives preferred the limited suffrage: as Brian Harrison describes it,
they 'frequently stressed the absurdity of a situation whereby the
educated and well-to-do lady was excluded from the franchise
which was enjoyed by her ignorant and propertyless gardener'.[57]
But others stuck to a primitive anti-feminism. Some anti-
suffragists of all hues disliked reformers as a breed, and viewed
them as irritants regardless of their particular passions. Others
continued the nineteenth-century willingness to allocate women
to local social work as a proper outlet; a municipal vote had been
granted in 1869, and, building on this, in 1910 the women's
society of the Anti-Suffrage League decided to encourage 'the
principle of the representation of women on municipal and other
bodies concerned with the domestic and social affairs of the
community'.[58] Criticism from the left similarly reworked earlier

positions. For some marxists – here, Belfort Bax – suffragism represented an intolerable battle of sex versus class:

> The anti-man agitation forms a capital red herring for drawing the popular scent of class opposition by substituting sex antagonism in its place.[59]

From part of the labour movement, antipathy sprang from the suspicion that organised feminism, if enfranchised, might clash yet more vehemently with the leading trade unions over the restriction of women's paid work by means of protective legislation, to which some feminist tendencies were opposed. Or, as the radical John Bright announced, in a dismissal which still stalks feminism today, 'Women are not a class.'[60]

*   *   *

Right up to 1928, the year of the quietly bestowed universal franchise, the range of anti-suffrage opinion continued to be broad; conservative and progressive feeling could often coincide on the supposition that 'women' were a unified constituency, awash with sex-specific characteristics. From the 1830s' raising of women's candidacy in radical, Owenite and Saint-Simonian discussion onwards, 'women' as a collectivity had been argued, stretched, dismembered, dragged hither and thither, re-aligned in every possible direction. Philosophical ideas about femininity could be either allied to, or set against, tactical platforms. The awkwardness of 'women' as political aspirants was constantly and violently exposed. Given this impossibility of speaking straightforwardly for 'women' in any unencumbered manner, how was it that the suffrage was ever won in Britain? Only by hesitant and piecemeal means. Changes to the Lords in 1911 made adult suffrage a more tangible prospect; manhood suffrage crept on by stages; at least some sections of the Labour Party began to accept that under the umbrella of the new electoral reforms women's suffrage could also be included. But these vulnerable beginnings were interrupted by the outbreak of war, and even after it in 1918, full adult suffrage was restricted to men; some women were admitted, not as property-owners but as over-30-year-olds who were university graduates or the wives of local government electors, or electors themselves; all women were not enfranchised for another decade.[61]

I have drawn on a limited instance of the difficulties faced by feminisms of whatever hue in proposing 'women', even with qualifying restrictions. A full and comparative history of international suffrage would illuminate different dismemberments of 'women' – thus, in America, race disrupted the homogeneity of sex as property did in Britain. The tactical and political torments endured by different national feminisms varied accordingly. But a common central problem remained. It is rarely, if ever, the case that all women will step forward as completely unified candidates for emancipation; and then 'women' *en masse* are so heavily endowed in advance with the alleged psyche of their species that they are ruled out. Just as 'women', they are impossible; while as 'some women', they are inegalitarian. Women in later-nineteenth-century Britain *were* 'sexual difference' incarnate as a group; the selfsame group that sought to plunge its sometimes oppressive distinctiveness into the generality of all voters. Yet where that liability, the ascribed unity of 'women', did collapse under the demarcating weight of property ownership, that was still of no advantage to the suffragists. They could not try to usher in the franchise by cheerfully arguing that differences among 'women' broke down their supposedly monstrous unity, since these very divisions could be turned against suffragism too. 'Some women' implied a stagnant Toryism. At the same time, any reactive tactics of *realpolitik* had to contend with the constant background of a devastating homogeneity of 'women' as creatures of a separate culture and sphere. The introduction of fresh differences among women only exaggerated the fundamental impasse of absolute difference.

This is illustrated by, for instance, the failure of the suffragist claim that the very psychic distinctiveness of 'women' might well qualify them for the vote, because it fairly amended the national temperamental and judicious balance of the existing electorate. It was only when the hundred flowers of ascribed differences had wilted under the creeping exhaustions of time, repetitions, and covert reform that all women were, in a subdued fashion, eventually admitted. Meanwhile, suffragist feminisms had for many decades been stretched to breaking-point on that wellworn Procrustean bed of a 'sexed versus human', or a 'differentiated versus inclusive', democracy. While the manifold political labours for the suffrage were both imperative and eventually satisfied, the abyss between 'women' and 'human' opened under them at every turn.

There was no way in which some synthesising feminism could have arched over this; the ambiguity of 'women' could not be resolved. On the contrary, what the feminist demand for the vote did was to lay it bare.

But could there not still be, in principle or under other more propitious circumstances, a new feminist advocacy of women; one which would finally succeed in dissolving this ambiguity? In my concluding discussion, I will suggest that this is an impossible longing – and maintain that to say so is in the interests of feminist thought and politics.

5

Bodies, Identities,
Feminisms

Instead of interrogating a category, we will interrogate
a woman. It will at least be more agreeable.
(E. P. Thompson, *The Poverty of Theory, or An Orrery
of Errors*, 1978)

> Let it be a care
> How man or child
> Be called man or child,
> Or woman, woman.
> (Laura Riding, 'Care in Calling', *The Poems
> of Laura Riding*, 1938)

In my first chapter there were allusions to what I called the peculiar
temporalities of 'women'. But what are the consequences of this
for feminism; what does it mean to insist that 'women' are only
sometimes 'women', and wouldn't this suggestion undercut
feminism anyway? As part of my argument that it would not, we
could start with a fairly straightforward version of what this
temporality might be.

That is, that it's not possible to live twenty-four hours a day
soaked in the immediate awareness of one's sex. Gendered self-
consciousness has, mercifully, a flickering nature. Yet even here
there are at once some puzzles; because to be hit by the intrusions
of bodily being – to be caught out by the start of menstruation, for
instance – is just not the same as being caught up unexpectedly in
'being a woman'. Only at some secondary stage of reflection
induced by something else, some ironic juxtaposition perhaps,
would your thought about your body's abrupt interruption
become, 'Now, maddeningly, I'm pushed into this female gender.'
But what about a classic example of another kind of precipitation
into a sexed self-consciousness? You walk down a street wrapped
in your own speculations; or you speed up, hell-bent on getting to
the shops before they close: a car slows down, a shout comments

96

on your expression, your movement; or there's a derisively hissed remark from the pavement. You have indeed been seen 'as a woman', and violently reminded that your passage alone can spark off such random sexual attraction-cum-contempt, that you can be a spectacle when the last thing on your mind is your own embodiedness. But again, the first thought here, surely, is not, 'Now, humiliatingly, I've become a woman', but rather that you have been positioned antagonistically as a woman-thing, objectified as a distortion.

So in both of these examples, the description of 'suddenly becoming your sex' would be too secondary to be accurate. In the first case, the leakage of blood means that the sovereignty exercised by your hormonal cycle has gone and done it again. You might view this badly timed event as your being taken up – or thrown down – into your sex, but you need not do so. In the second case, the mastery not of 'nature' but of 'man' is so leadenly at work that it has pushed you into what leftist sociologists would once have called an alienated self-recognition. Are there, then, any readily available senses in which a simple conception of 'being a woman at times' can hold good? Are there moments when some, as it were, non-ideological kind of woman-ness irrupts, such that you are for that moment a woman unironically and without compromise?

Someone might well retort, against my dark examples, that the experiences of sexual happiness or of childbearing might furnish resonantly optimistic ways of taking up 'being a woman now'. And that these instances can affirm some solidarities among women; that there are such positive elements to being a woman that only a joyless Puritan could miss them; and that it is exaggeratedly pessimistic to characterise the mutual recognition of woman-ness as merely the exchanged glances of those cornered in the same cells by the epithet 'woman'.

There is an obstinate, perhaps intractable, difficulty inherent in this argument, to which I'll return soon. For the moment, it seems to me that even the apparently simplest, most innocent ways in which one becomes temporarily a woman *are not* darting returns to a category in a natural and harmless state, but are something else: adoptions of, or precipitations into, a designation there in advance, a characterisation of 'woman'. This holds true for even the warmest, the most benign congratulation on one's being 'a real woman'. And while there is indeed a phenomenology of inhabit-

ing a sex, the swaying in and out of it is more like ventures among
descriptions than like returns to a founding sexed condition.

So to speak about the individual temporality of being a woman
is really to speak about movements between the many temporalities of a designation. And as this designation alters historically, so do these myriad possibilities assume different shapes.
'Women' as a collective noun has suffered its changes, as the
chapters above have suggested. If we look at these historical
temporalities of 'women' in the same light as the individual
temporalities, then once again no originary, neutral and inert
'woman' lies there like a base behind the superstructural vacillations. Some characterisation or other is eternally in play. The
question then for a feminist history is to discover whose, and with
what effects. This constant characterising also generates the political dilemma for feminism, which – necessarily landed with
'women' – has no choice but to work with or against different
versions of the same wavering collectivity.

Is 'women', then, an eternally compromised noun? Suppose it is
admitted that even the statistician and the anatomist are up to
something when they amass 'women' for their purposes; aren't,
say, medical discoveries about preventing cervical cancer examples of a valuable concentration on 'women'? Or legislation for
equal rights and educational chances, which must name the social
grouping that they help? Or feminist invocations of 'women',
which, alert to the differences between them, call for courage and
solidarity within and between their pluralities? Granted, it would
be wildly perverse to deny that there can be *any* progressive
deployments of 'women' – all the achievements of emancipation
and campaigning would be obliterated in that denial. My aim is
different – it is to emphasise that inherent shakiness of the
designation 'women' which exists prior to both its revolutionary
and conservative deployments, and which is reflected in the
spasmodic and striking coincidences of leftist and rightist propositions about the family or female nature. The cautionary point of
this emphasis is far from being anti-feminist. On the contrary, it
is to pin down this instability as the lot of feminism, which
resolves certain perplexities in the history of feminism and its
vacillations, but also points to its potentially inexhaustible flexibil-
ity in pursuing its aims. This would include a capacity for a lively
and indeed revivifying irony about this 'women' who is the
subject of all tongues. A political movement possessed of
reflexivity and an ironic spirit would be formidable indeed.

To be named as a woman can be the precondition for some kinds of solidarity. Political rhetorics which orchestrate an identity of 'women' or 'mothers' may generate refusals from their ostensible targets. So, to the well-known Lacanian formula – that there's no becoming a subject without having to endure some corresponding subjection – we could add, a little more optimistically, that there's no becoming a subject without the generation, sooner or later, of a contesting politics of that subject. Nevertheless, this revision doesn't get near the heart of the problem introduced at the beginning of this chapter, of the 'positive' aspects of 'women' as a collectivity.

There is a wish among several versions of Anglo-American feminism to assert the real underlying unities among women, and of the touchstone of 'women's experience'. It is as if this powerful base could guarantee both the integrity and the survival of militant feminism. Other schools, sometimes influenced by readings of Luce Irigaray, emphasise their belief in the necessity of a philosophy which includes the distinctiveness of women's bodies. Despite their different genealogies, both this specifying the feminine and the stress on 'experience' share the conviction that there is a real or potential common essence to being a woman, which must not suffer eclipse. The now familiar device for challenging the essentialism from a feminist perspective attacks its false universality in representing the experiences of, usually, middle-class white western women as if they embraced all womankind. But this move to replace the tacit universal with the qualified 'some women's experience' is both necessary yet in the end inadequate. Below the newly pluralised surfaces, the old problems still linger.

There is no gainsaying the forcefulness of the moment of recognition, the 'but that's me!' of some described experience, which, if the political possibilities are there, will pull some women together into a declared feminism. Perhaps it is not so much the 'experience' that is the puzzle which persists after the pluralising correction has been made, but the 'women's experience'. The phrase works curiously, for it implies that the experiences originate with the women, and it masks the likelihood that instead these have accrued to women not by virtue of their womanhood alone, but as traces of domination, whether natural or political. And while these may indeed pertain uniquely to one sex, they can hardly be used to celebrate or underwrite the state of being a woman without many gloomier qualifications. But it is virtually impossible for feminism to unpick 'women's experience' to its own satisfaction.

This is because, in its historical analysis, social upheavals produce the experiences; but then, rather than appealing to the altered 'women' who are the constructions or the outcome of these, feminism, a product itself of these revolutionary processes, appeals for solidarity to an embryonic consciousness of women. Because of its drive towards a political massing together of women, feminism can never wholeheartedly dismantle 'women's experience', however much this category conflates the attributed, the imposed, and the lived, and then sanctifies the resulting mélange.

But do we always need the conviction of unifying experience to ground a rallying cry? Donna Haraway has denied this:

> We do not need a totality in order to work well. The feminist dream of a common language, like all dreams for a perfectly faithful naming of experience, is a totalizing and imperialist one. In that sense, dialectics too is a dream language, longing to resolve contradiction.[1]

She pursues her attack on that spectrum of identities and identifications which constitute some contemporary feminist thought:

> Feminisms and Marxisms have run aground on Western epistemological alternatives to construct a revolutionary subject from the perspective of a hierarchy of oppressions and/or a latent position of moral superiority, innocence, and greater closeness to nature. With no available original dream of a common language or original symbiosis promising protection from hostile 'masculine' separation, but written into the play of a text that has no finally privileged reading or salvation history, to recognise 'oneself' as fully implicated in the world frees us of the need to root politics in identification, vanguard parties, purity, and mothering.[2]

It might be objected that there are marxisms which refuse wholeness, and feminisms which refuse identification – but if we let these qualifications pass, there is still a question as to whether this vivid recommendation to a radical pluralism is able to cope with the fundamental dilemmas lodged in the category 'women'. It vaults over them here, but they must return – or they will do so for as long as sexual division is a bifurcation of the discursive world, a state of affairs that it's hard to envisage withering away. It is that obstinate core of identification, purity, and mothering which helps to underpin the appeal to 'women's experience' – and that core is the concept of the female body.

* * *

Here we are on notoriously difficult ground. Hard, indeed, to speak against the body. Even if it is allowed that the collective 'women' may be an effect of history, what about biology, materiality? Surely, it is argued, those cannot be evaporated into time. And from the standpoint of feminism, what has always been lacking is a due recognition of the specificity of women's bodies, sexual difference as lived. Indeed, Simone de Beauvoir – she who, ironically, has been so often upbraided for paying no attention to precisely what she does name here – wrote in *The Second Sex*:

> In the sexual act and in maternity not only time and strength but also essential values are involved for woman. Rationalist materialism tries in vain to disregard this dramatic aspect of sexuality.[3]

Several contemporary feminisms also set themselves against what they believe to be a damaging indifference to the powerful distinct realities of the body. Here Elizabeth Gross sets out her understanding of the Irigarayan conception:

> All bodies must be male or female, and the particularities, specificities and differences of each need to be recognised and represented in specific terms. The social and patriarchal disavowal of the specificity of women's bodies is a function, not only of discriminatory social practices, but, more insidiously, of the phallocentrism invested in the régimes of knowledge – science, philosophy, the arts – which function only because and with the effect of the submersion of women under male categories, values and norms. For Irigaray, the reinscription, through discourses, of a positive, autonomous body for women is to render disfunctional all forms of knowledge that have hitherto presented themselves as neutral, objective or perspective-less.[4]

If, for the moment, we take up this conviction about the political-analytic force of women's bodies and lead it towards history, then our question becomes – In what ways have these social and patriarchal 'disavowals' functioned, and how could the subdued bodies of women be restored in a true form? Do the existing social histories of the female body answer that? They do not. We may leaf through voyeuristic and sensational catalogues of revulsion. That is not to deny that, could they escape being charmed by the morbid, the histories of trained, exploited, or distorted flesh – of bodies raped, circumcised, infected, ignorantly treated in childbirth or subjected to constant pregnancies – would carry some moral force.[5] In respect of the developed countries at least, such accounts would suggest that women are less relentlessly caught in physical toils than they were, as pregnancy can be restricted and gynaecological hazards are far less catastrophic – that in this sense, women can spend less of their lives awkwardly *in* their bodies. But even this fragile assumption of progress can be qualified if we recall that contraception was rarely a complete mystery even when the physiology of reproduction was not deciphered, and that medical Whiggishness must be shaken by many examples – the exhaustion of over-used antibiotics, the ascent of new viral strains, the deeply undemocratic distribution of resources, the advancing technologies of international genocide.

So to the history of the body as a narrative of morbidity and its defeats, we could contrast a historical sociology of the body. This would worry about the management of populations, about social policies drawing on demography or eugenics, about malnutrition caused by economic policy in another hemisphere, the epidemiology of industrial and nuclear pollution, and so forth. Yet in all this, both 'the body' and 'women's bodies' will have slipped away as objects, and become instead almost trace phenomena which are produced by the wheelings-about of great technologies and politics. Is this simply the predictable end of that peculiar hypostatisation, 'the body'? Perhaps it must always be transmuted into bodies in the plural, which are not only marked and marred by famine, or gluttony, destitution or plenty, hazard or planning, but are also shaped and created by them. 'The body' is not, for all its corporeality, an originating point nor yet a terminus; it is a result or an effect.

And yet this train of thought doesn't satisfy our original question of the bodies of women in history. Even a gender-specific historical sociology would somehow miss the point. For instance, we could consider what an account of *men's* bodies would look

like; it would include historical descriptions of sex-related ill-
nesses, heart disease, lung cancer and the statistical challenge here
from women; the history of soldiery, war slaughter, conscription;
of virility as a concept, of Sparta; of the greater vulnerability of the
male foetus; of narcissism and its failures; of disabling conditions
of work, of mining accidents; of the invention of the male
homosexual as a species-being. A history of prostitution but this
time written from the side of the clients, of contraception written
from the side of the fathers – to add to the histories of bodily
endurance, triumphant musculature, or the humiliations of the
feebler of frame. All this and more could count up the male body
in history, its frailties and its enjoyments, analogously to
women's. Yet the sum of the two parts, men and women, would
still not produce a satisfying total of 'the body', now democrati-
cally analysed with a proper regard to sexual difference.

What would have gone wrong, then, in the search? A chain of
unease remains: that anyone's body is – the classifications of
anatomy apart – only periodically either lived or treated as sexed,
therefore the gendered division of human life into bodily life
cannot be adequate or absolute. Only at times will the body
impose itself or be arranged as that of a woman or a man. So that if
we set out to track the bodies of women in history, we would
assume in advance that which really we needed to catch, instead,
on the wing of its formulation. Neither the body marked with
time, nor the sexed body marked with time, are the right concepts
here. For the impress of history as well as of individual temporality is to establish the body itself as lightly or as heavily gendered,
or as indifferent, and for that to run in and out of the eye of 'the
social'. It's more of a question of tracing the (always anatomically
gendered) body as it is differently established and interpreted as
sexed within different periods. If female bodies are thought of as
perenially such, as constant and even embodiments of sexed
being, that is a misconception which carries risks. If it leads to
feminist celebrations of the body as female, which intoxicatingly
forget the temporality and malleability of gendered existence, at
the same time it makes the feminist critique of, say, the instru-
mental positioning of women's bodies all the harder to develop
coherently, because this critique needs some notion of temporality
too. It could be claimed that a characteristic of the sadist's gaze is
to fix and freeze its object, to insist on absolute difference, to
forbid movement.

There is a further reason for unease with the sufficiency of a historical sociology of the body, sexed or not. In a strong sense the body is a concept, and so is hardly intelligible unless it is read in relation to whatever else supports it and surrounds it. Indeed the queer neutrality of the phrase 'the body' in its strenuous colour-lessness suggests that something is up. We could speculate that some of the persistent draw of this 'the body' lies in the tacit promise to ground the sexual, to make intimacy more readily decipherable, less evanescent. But then this enticement is under-cut by the fact that the very location of 'the sexual' in the body is itself historically mutable. And 'the body' is never above – or below – history.

This is visible in the degree, for instance, to which it is held co-extensive with the person; to which the mind–body distinction is in play, if at all; to which the soul is held to have the capacity to dominate the flesh. If the contemporary body is usually consi-dered as sexed, exactly what this means now is in part the residue remaining after a long historical dethronement of the soul's pow-ers, which in turn has swayed the balance of sexed nature. The modern western body is what the soul has thoroughly vacated (in favour, for some, of the unconscious). But here there is no sym-metry between the sexes, because we can show that 'sex' expanded differently into the old fields of soul and body in a different way for 'women'. I suggested earlier that the eighteenth-century remnants of the soul were flooded with the womanly body, preparing the way for the nineteenth-century naturalising of the species Woman. Any history of how far 'the body' has been read as the measure of the human being would have to include this – how far 'the body' has been read as co-extensive with the gender of its bearer.

Some philosophical writings now hint that 'the body' does have the status of a realm of underlying truth, and try to rescue it from medicine or sociology by making it vivid again. Sebastiano Tim-panaro attempts this for socialism in his On Materialism.[6] And Michel Foucault, at points in his History of Sexuality, treats 'bodies and their pleasures' as touchstones of an anarchic truth, innocent brute clarities which are then scored through with the strategies of bio-technical management from on high.[7] But elsewhere in his work there is nothing of a last court of appeal in the body. On the contrary, in the essay, 'Nietzsche, Genealogy, History', he writes:

> The body is the inscribed surface of events (traced by language and dissolved by ideas), the locus of a dissociated self (adopting

the illusion of a substantial unity), and a volume in perpetual disintegration. Genealogy, as an analysis of descent, is thus situated within the articulation of the body and history. Its task is to expose a body totally imprinted by history and the process of history's destruction of the body.[8]

The integrity of the body's claim to afford a starting-point for analysis is refused:

> 'Effective' history differs from traditional history in being without constraints. Nothing in man – not even his body – is sufficiently stable to serve as the basis for self-recognition or for understanding other men.[9]

This Foucauldian body is a deliquescing effect; composed but constantly falling away from itself. What if the 'man' attached to it is erased, and 'woman' set there instead? Has history 'totally imprinted' the bodies of women in different ways?

One train of thought must answer yes. That women's bodies become women's bodies only as they are caught up in the tyrannies, the overwhelming incursions of both nature and man – or, more optimistically, that there are also vehement pleasures and delights to offset a history of unbridled and violent subjection. But to be faithful to the suggestion that 'the body' is really constantly altering as a concept means that we must back off from the supposition that women's bodies are systematically and exhaustively different, that they are unified in an integral otherness. Instead we would need to maintain that women only sometimes live in the flesh distinctively of women, as it were, and this is a function of historical categorisations as well as of an individual daily phenomenology. To say that is by no means to deny that because of the cyclical aspects of female physiology, there may be a greater overall degree of slipping in and out of the consciousness of the body for many women. But even this will always be subject to different interpretations, and nothing more radical than the facts of intermittent physiology really holds the bodies of women together.

Where they are dragged together, a sort of miserable sexual democracy may obtain – of malnutrition, for instance – although then they may well move from being starved bodies to being starved sexed bodies as amenorrhea sets in. But these are rare constructions which do produce 'women's bodies' as the victims of shared sufferings. Conditions of deprivation, of sex-specific hard labour, do also pull together the bent backs of women, but then it is the sexual division of labour which has made the partition – not a natural bodily unity. Another kind of massing of potentially maternal bodies belongs to demographic policies, although even here 'nature' is remote. Of course, if women did not have the capacity of childbearing they could not be arrayed by natalist or anti-natalist plans into populations to be cajoled or managed. But the point is that irrespective of natural capacities, only some prior lens which intends to focus on 'women's bodies' is going to set them in such a light. The body becomes visible *as* a body, and *as* a female body, only under some particular gaze – including that of politics.

So the sexed body is not something reliably constant, which can afford a good underpinning for the complications of the thousand discourses on 'women'. How and when even the body will be understood and lived as gendered, or indeed as a body at all, is not fully predictable. Again this isn't only a function of an individual phenomenology but of a historical and political phenomenology. There is no deep natural collectivity of women's bodies which precedes some subsequent arrangement of them through history or biopolitics. If the body is an unsteady mark, scarred in its long decay, then the sexed body too undergoes a similar radical temporality, and more transitory states.

Then what is the attraction of the category of the body at all? For those feminist philosophies which espouse it, it promises a means of destabilising the tyranny of systematic blindness of sexual difference. It has to be conceded that such philosophies do not have to assume any naturally bestowed identity of women; the female body can be harshly characterised from above. This is demonstrated through Elizabeth Gross's exposition of the Irigayan schema, a clear, sympathetic account of the feminist reception of that work:

Psychical, social and interpersonal meanings thus mark the body, and through it, the identities or interiority of sexed objects. The female body is inscribed socially, and most often, individually experienced as a lacking, incomplete or inadequate body . . . Women's oppression is generated in part by these systems of patriarchal morphological inscription – that is, by a patriarchal symbolic order – or part by internalised, psychic representations of this inscribed body, and in part as a result of the different behaviours, values and norms that result from these different morphologies and psychologies. Irigaray's aim . . . is to speak about a positive model or series of representations of femininity by which the female body may be positively marked, which in its turn may help establish the conditions necessary for the production of new kinds of discourse, new forms of knowledge and new modes of practice.[10]

It is the conclusion here which worries me – that the goal is a fresh and autonomous femininity, voiced in a revolutionary new language, to speak a non-alienated being of woman. Indeed the 'woman' we have available is severely damaged. But for myself – in common with many other feminists, but unlike many others again – I would not seek the freshly conceived creature, the revelatory Woman we have not yet heard. She is an old enough project, whose repeated failures testify to the impossibility of carving out a truly radical space; the damage flows from the very categorisation 'woman' which is and has always been circumscribed in advance from some quarter or other, rendering the ideal of a purely self-representing 'femininity' implausible. A true independence here would only be possible when all existing ideas of sexual difference had been laid to rest; but then 'woman', too, would be buried.

Such reflections undo the ambition to retrieve women's bodies from their immersions beneath 'male categories, values and norms'. The body circulates inexorably among the other categories which sometimes arrange it in sexed ranks, sometimes not. For the concept 'women's bodies' is opaque, and like 'women' it is always in some juxtaposition to 'human' and to 'men'. If this is envisaged as a triangle of identifications, then it is rarely an equilateral triangle in which both sexes are pitched at matching distances from the apex of the human. And the figure is further skewed by the asymmetries of the histories of the sexes as concepts as well as their present disjointedness. If 'women' after the late seventeenth century undergoes intensified feminising, this change does not occur as a linear shift alone, as if we had moved from mercifully less of 'women' through a later excess of them. Other notions which redefine understandings of the person have their influential upheavals: Reason, Nature, the Unconscious, among many. The periodic hardenings of 'women' don't happen alone or in any necessary continuum (as any history of individualism would need to take into account).

*   *   *

For 'women' are always differently re-membered, and the gulf between them and the generally human will be more or less thornily intractable. One measure of that gulf is the depth of 'women's' resonances. Is it so highly charged, just as a noun, that it is impassably remote from the human? Can it be claimed that the collective 'women' possesses a virtually metaphorical force, in the way that the theatrical Woman does? And if it does, this force would change. Linguistic studies of the 1950s contemplated the ranges of metaphor. William Empson examined I. A. Richards' proposal that all language was indeed radically metaphorical, but found this wanting; 'cat', Empson objected, was a hopeless candidate for metaphor status.[11] The 'woman–beauty' equation was one which Empson would allow; and he believed that such a tacit metaphor as 'woman' carried a 'pregnant' use in which the word was full with its own extra weight. The emotive colouring of some words was, as other linguists described it, an integral part of their signification. But where there could be fullness, so there could be contraction; the historical 'hardening of a convention' might narrow the range of a word. Here Empson offered the example of Chastity, which gradually became restricted in its reference to women's conduct. This alteration came about, he thought, because 'what changes in the language are, so to speak, practical policies'. If it were true that 'a word can become a "compacted doctrine" or even that all words are compacted doctrines inherently' then it would be vital to grasp these means 'by which our language is continually thrusting doctrines upon us, perhaps very ill-considered ones'.[12] Perhaps, Empson concluded, this risky power could be caught at its work through those analyses which had interested I. A. Richards – of the interactions 'between a word's Sense and its Emotion or Gesture'.[13]

To adopt Empson's phrase, the evolutions of 'women' must offer a good instance of a changing 'compacted doctrine'. Is the variant with which post-Enlightenment feminism must tangle, woman as almost an anthropological species-being, nevertheless so impacted that it dooms feminism to being a kind of oppositional anthropology to protect its own kin? Or can we look for evolutions of 'women' itself? Rather than this, Julia Kristeva has suggested that modern European feminism, because of its very invocation of 'women', is itself a temporary form which must wither away. She has described this feminism as in some ways 'but a *moment* in the thought of that anthropomorphic identity which currently blocks the horizon of the discursive and scientific adventure of our species'.[14] So, in her account, 'woman' has merely inherited that baggage of drawbacks belonging to the generic 'man'. European feminism, trading in this debased currency 'women', has turned into a renewed form of the tedious old anthropomorphism – into a gynomorphism which is equally suspect. In the fullness of revolutionary time, it too would have to be transcended.

Meanwhile she characterises two strands of contemporary feminism. One associates women, using spatial references, to the timelessly maternal. Cyclical, monumental temporalities are allied to an idea of femaleness. As with James Joyce's antithesis, 'Father's time, mother's species', these take their distance from linear, historical notions of time. The result, she writes, is that 'female subjectivity as it gives itself up to intuition becomes a problem with respect to a certain conception of time; time as project, teleology, linear and prospective unfolding; time as departure, progression, and arrival – in other words, the time of history'.[15]

This tendency is perfectly consonant with the sensibilities of a newer feminism which lacks interest in the 'values of a rationality dominant in the nation state'.[16] Here it departs from its antecedents, the egalitarian feminism which had spoken to the state, especially on family policy matters. Nevertheless this newer philosophy, despite its theoretical unwillingness to be dealing with political history, in practice often tied in with the older strand. A curious eclecticism, as Kristeva describes it, resulted – a theory of timeless sexual difference which was none the less embedded in history, an '*insertion* into history and the radical *refusal* of the subjective limitations imposed by this history's time on an experiment carried out in the name of the irreducible difference'.[17]

This is a good characterisation too of the history which holds that an eternal sexual antagonism will always be re-enacted in changing skirmishes, as if men and women are the same actors wearing different costumes from scene to scene but whose clashes are always the same. Kristeva takes the opposite stance: 'the very dichotomy man/woman as an opposition between two rival entities may be understood as belonging to metaphysics'.[18] This must be dismantled through 'the demassification of the problem of difference, which would imply, in a first phase, an apparent de-dramatisation of the "flight to the death" between rival groups and thus between the sexes'.[19]

How, though, to carry out this programme of lowering the dramatic stakes? Not, she argues, by aiming at a 'reconciliation' between the warring sexes, but by relocating the struggle in the opposite arena. That would be 'in the very place where it operates with the maximum intransigence, in other words, in personal and social identity itself, so as to make it disintegrate in its very nucleus'.[20] Such a strategy of disintegration would include intensifying aesthetic practices which bring out 'the relativity of his/her symbolic as well as biological existence'.[21] There is a true radicalism in this attempt to undo given identities, to go beyond the policy of creating counter-identifications. It is evident that 'women' do undergo an excessive bestowal of all too many identities, and forcing new content into the old category is a doomed project. But does it follow that a radical policy of harassing tediously entrenched namings must also hold feminism to be a transitional aspect of what is to be attacked? Certainly if all that feminism could ever manage was a parrot-like reiteration of sexual fixity – it has to be admitted that at worst some versions are that – then its dissolution would be a blessing. But in its past and in its present, feminism is infinitely more ambiguous and sophisticated than that parody allows. Only by ignoring the twists and turns of its history can it be seen as a monotonous proponent of a simple sexual difference, or of an unshaded idea of equality.

Julia Kristeva's recommendation is a bold stroke – that the only revolutionary road will slice through the current confusions to bypass 'women' as an anthropomorphic stumbling-block. But this would only follow if you assume that the identity of 'women' is really coherent, so that you are faced only with the options of revering it, or abandoning it for its hopeless antagonistic conservatism, as she proposes. And it would also only follow if you had an extraordinary faith in the powers of 'aesthetic practices' to erode, for example, the sexual division of labour. A policy of minimising 'women' could be more plausibly pursued by going through the instances of the categorisation in all their diversity to see what these effect, rather than longing to obliterate 'women' wholesale, as if this massification really did represent a unity. But such a scrutiny would not be likely to reach some welcome point of termination. For as long as the sexes are socially distinguished, 'women' will be nominated in their apartness, so that sexual division will always be liable to conflation with some fundamental ontological sexual difference. So feminism, the reaction to this state of affairs, cannot be merely transitional, and a true post-feminism can never arrive.

But if feminism can't be fairly characterised as a passing cloud which heralds the dawn of an ultimate sexual translucency, then neither must it be understood to name untroubled solidities of women. It cannot be a philosophy of 'the real'. Given that the anatomically female person far outstrips the ranges of the limiting label 'woman', then she can always say in all good faith, 'here I am not a woman', meaning 'in this contracting description I cannot recognize myself; there is more to this life than the designation lets on, and to interpret every facet of existence as really gendered produces a claustrophobia in me; I am not drawn by the charm of an always sexually distinct universe'.

Nevertheless, modern feminism, because it deals with the conditions of groups, is sociological in its character as it is in its historical development. It cannot escape the torments which spring from speaking for a collectivity. The members of any exhorted mass – whether of a race, a class, a nation, a bodily state, a sexual persuasion – are always apt to break out of its corrals to re-align themselves elsewhere. Indeed, the very indeterminacy of the span of 'being a woman' can form the concealed subject-matter of a political sociology of women which is interested in their 'stages'.

These difficulties can't be assuaged by appeals to the myriad types and conditions of women on this earth. They are not a matter of there being different *sorts of* women, but of the effects of the designation, 'women'. Criticisms of white educated Western feminism for generalising from its own experiences have been strongly voiced, and have had their proper impact. Yet however decisively ethnocentricity is countered, and the diversities of women in race and class allowed, even the most sophisticated political sociology is not going to be concerned with the historical crystallisations of sexed identities. Modern feminism, which in its sociological aspects is landed with the identity of women as an achieved fact of history and epistemology, can only swing between asserting or refusing the completeness of this given identity.

But both the 'special needs' of women as different or the desired 'equality' of women as similar may be swamped by the power of the categorisation to defeat such fractures within it.

*   *   *

Equality; difference; 'different but equal' – the history of feminism since the 1790s has zigzagged and curved through these incomplete oppositions upon which it is itself precariously erected. This swaying motion need not be a wonder, nor a cause for despair. If feminism is the voicing of 'women' from the side of 'women', then it cannot but act out the full ambiguities of that category. This reflection reduces some of the sting and mystery of feminism's ceaseless oscillations, and allows us to prophesy its next incarnations. Yet to adopt such a philosophical resignation to the vagaries of a movement doomed to veer through eternity is cold comfort, perhaps. What does it imply for the practice of feminist politics? And if indeed the label 'woman' is inadequate, that it is neither possible nor desirable to live solidly inside any sexed designation, then isn't that its own commentary on the unwillingness of many to call themselves feminists? It explains, too, the exhaustion with reiterations about 'women' which must afflict the most dedicated feminist. Surely it's not uncommon to be tired, to long to be free of the merciless guillotines of those gendered invocations thumping down upon all speech and writing, to long, like Winifred Holtby, for 'an end of the whole business . . . the very name of feminist . . . to be about the work in which my real interests lie'.[22]

Does all of this mean, then, that the better programme for feminism now would be – to minimise 'women'? To cope with the oscillations by so downplaying the category that insisting on either differences or identities would become equally untenable? My own suggestions grind to a halt here, on a territory of pragmatism. I'd argue that it is compatible to suggest that 'women' don't exist – while maintaining a politics of 'as if they existed' – since the world behaves as if they unambiguously did. So that official suppositions and conservative popular convictions will need to be countered constantly by redefinitions of 'women'. Such challenges to 'how women are' can throw sand in the eyes of the founding categorisations and attributions, ideally disorientating them. But the risk here is always that the very iteration of the afflicted category serves, maliciously, not to undo it but to underwrite it. The intimacies between consenting to be a subject and undergoing subjection are so great that even to make demands as an oppositional subject may well extend the trap, wrap it furiously around oneself. Yet this is hardly a paralysing risk, if it's recognised.

Sometimes it will be a soundly explosive tactic to deny, in the face of some thoughtless depiction, that there *are* any 'women'. But at other times, the entrenchment of sexed thought may be too deep for this strategy to be understood and effective. So feminism must be agile enough to say, 'Now we will be "women" – but now we will be persons, not these "women".' And, in practice, what sounds like a rigid opposition – between a philosophical correctness about the indeterminacy of the term, and a strategical willingness to clap one's feminist hand over one's theoretical mouth and just get on with 'women' where necessary – will loosen. A category may be at least conceptually shaken if it is challenged and refurbished, instead of only being perversely strengthened by repetition. For instance, to argue that it's untrue that women workers freely gravitate towards some less-well-paid jobs because these fit their natural inclinations, does indeed leave the annoyingly separable grouping, 'women workers', untouched, but it also successfully muddies the content of that term.[23] And the less that 'women workers' can be believed to have a fixed nature, as distinct from neglected needs because of their domestic responsibilities, the more it will be arguable that only for some purposes can they be distinguished from all workers. Feminism can then join battle over which these purposes are to be. Of course this means that feminism must 'speak women', while at the same time, an acute awareness of its vagaries is imperative. Domestic concerns can easily be rewritten into a separate spheres familialism, as in some European countries in the 1930s; aggressive recuperations are always hovering near. So an active scepticism about the integrity of the sacred category 'women' would be no merely philosophical doubt to be stifled in the name of effective political action in the world. On the contrary, it would be a condition *for* the latter.

To be, or not to be, 'a woman'; to write or not 'as a woman'; to espouse an egalitarianism which sees sexed manifestations as blocks on the road to full democracy; to love theories of difference which don't anticipate their own dissolution: these uncertainties are rehearsed endlessly in the history of feminism, and fought through within feminist-influenced politics. That 'women' is indeterminate and impossible is no cause for lament. It is what makes feminism; which has hardly been an indiscriminate embrace anyway of the fragilities and peculiarities of the category. What these do demand is a willingness, at times, to shred this 'women' to bits – to develop a speed, foxiness, versatility. The temporalities of 'women' are like the missing middle term of Aristotelian logic; while it's impossible to thoroughly be a woman, it's also impossible never to be one. On such shifting sands feminism must stand and sway. Its situation in respect of the sexed categories recalls Merleau-Ponty's description of another powerful presence: 'There is no outstripping of sexuality any more than there is any sexuality enclosed within itself. No one is saved, and no one is totally lost.'[24]

Notes and References

1 Does a Sex have a History?

1. See Jacqueline Rose, 'Introduction – II', in J. Mitchell and J. Rose (eds), *Feminine Sexuality, Jacques Lacan and the École Freudienne*, London: Macmillan, 1982.
2. See Stephen Heath, 'Male Feminism', *Dalhousie Review*, no. 64, 2 (1986).
3. Jacques Derrida, *Spurs; Nietzsche's Styles*, Chicago: University of Chicago Press, 1978, pp. 51, 55.
4. See arguments in Lynne Segal, *Is the Future Female? Troubled Thoughts on Contemporary Feminism*, London: Virago, 1987.
5. Michel Foucault, 'Nietzsche, Genealogy, History', in *Language, Counter-Memory, Practice: Selected Essays and Interviews*, Donald F. Bouchard and Sherry Simon (eds and trans.), Ithaca: Cornell University Press, 1977, p. 162.
6. John Donne, 'The Relique', *Poems*, London, 1633.
7. See Joan Scott, 'L'Ouvrière! Mot Impie, Sordide . . .'': Women Workers in the Discourse of French Political Economy (1840–1860)', in P. Joyce (ed.), *The Historical Meanings of Work*, Cambridge University Press, 1987.
8. Jane Anger, 'Jane Anger her Protection for Women . . .', London, 1589, in Joan Goulianos (ed.), *By a Woman Writt, Literature from Six Centuries By and About Women*, Baltimore, Maryland: Penguin Books Inc., 1974, p. 25.
9. Ibid, p. 27.
10. Ibid, p. 28.
11. Mary Wollstonecraft, *A Vindication of the Rights of Woman*, 1792, Harmondsworth Penguin Books, 1982, p. 142.
12. Karl Marx, *Grundrisse*, Harmondsworth: Penguin Books, 1973, pp. 83, 496.
13. Ibid, pp. 104, 105.
14. Denise Riley, *War in the Nursery: Theories of the Child and Mother*, London: Virago, 1983, pp. 150–55, 195.

2 Progresses of the Soul

1. See the commentary by R. Hackforth to the *Phaedrus*, Cambridge University Press, 1952, pp. 75–7.

2. This is discussed by Genevieve Lloyd in *The Man of Reason: 'Male' and 'Female' in Western Philosophy*, London: Methuen, 1984, p. 37 onwards.

3. Peter Dronke, *Women Writers of the Middle Ages*, Cambridge University Press, 1984, pp. 180–81.

4. Ibid, p. 176.

5. Ibid, p. 175.

6. Ibid, p. 175.

7. Ibid, p. 219.

8. Ibid, p. 220.

9. Ian Maclean, *The Renaissance Notion of Woman; a study in the fortunes of scholasticism and medical science in European intellectual life*, Cambridge University Press, 1980, p. 1.

10. Ibid, p. 44.

11. Ibid, p. 30.

12. Ibid, p. 12.

13. Ibid, p. 30.

14. Ibid, pp. 87–8.

15. Ibid, p. 27.

16. In Margaret, Duchess of Newcastle, Part II of *A Treasure of Knowledge, OR, The Female Oracle*: included in *Poems on Several Subjects, both comical and serious in 2 parts*, by Alexander Nicol, Schoolmaster, Edinburgh, 1766.

17. (Margaret, Duchess of Newcastle): Lady Marchioness of Newcastle, 'Orations of Divers Sorts, accommodated to Divers Place', in *Divers Orations*, London, 1662, p. 228.

18. Ibid, p. 229.

19. Ibid, p. 229.

20. Ibid, p. 230.

21. Ibid, p. 231.

22. Ibid, p. 232.

23. Anon. The anonymous author is often held to be Mary Astell; or else Judith Drake. *An Essay in Defence of the Female Sex, in which are inserted the characters of A Pedant, A Squire, A Beau, A Vertuoso, A Poetaster, A City-Critick, &c*, Dedicated to Princess Anne of Denmark, 3rd Edition, London, 1697, p. 5.

24. Ibid, p. 5.

25. Ibid, Preface.

26. Ibid, p. 6.

27. Ibid, p. 11.

28. Ibid, p. 12.

29. Ibid, p. 14.

30. Ibid, p. 16.

31. Ibid, p. 18.

32. Ibid, p. 23.

33. Ibid, p. 56.

34. Mary Astell, *A Serious Proposal to the Ladies, for the Advancement of their True and Greatest Interest*, London, 1694. References here are to the 4th edition of 1697, p. 14.

35. Ibid, p. 29.
36. Ibid, p. 41.
37. Mary Astell, *Reflections upon Marriage*, London, 1700. References here are from the 3rd edition of 1706, p. 84.
38. Ibid, p. 85.
39. Ibid, p. 83.
40. Ibid, p. 91.
41. Ibid, Preface, not paginated.
42. Ibid, p. 31.
43. Ibid, p. 62.
44. Ibid, Preface.
45. Ibid, p. 47.
46. Ibid, p. 24.
47. Ibid, p. 48.
48. Ibid, p. 51.
49. Ibid, Preface.
50. Ibid, Preface.
51. This is elaborated by Dale van Kley, *The Jansenists and the Expulsion of the Jesuits from France, 1757–1765*, New Haven: Yale University Press, 1975, p. 9.
52. Jean-Jacques Rousseau, *La Nouvelle Héloise*, 1761. The references here are to the English translation of 1776 in four volumes by William Kenrick: *Eloisa*, p. 151.
53. Ibid, p. 152.
54. *Émile, ou de l'Education*, Amsterdam, 1762, 1780. References to the English edition, London: Everyman, 1905, p. 321.
55. Ibid, p. 322.
56. Ibid, p. 322.
57. Ibid, p. 324.
58. Ibid, p. 326.
59. Ibid, p. 324.
60. Ibid, p. 325.
61. Ibid, p. 326.
62. Ibid, p. 327.
63. Ibid, p. 349.
64. Ibid, p. 20.
65. Ibid, p. 13.
66. Ibid, p. 14.
67. See the discussion in Genevieve Lloyd, *Man of Reason*, passim.
68. Alasdair McIntyre, *A Short History of Ethics*, London: Routledge & Kegan Paul, 1967, p. 189.
69. Madame de Staël, *De La Littérature*, Paris, 1800. The references here are from *The Influence of Literature upon Society, translated from the French of Madame de Staël-Holstein*, in 2 volumes, London, 1812, pp. 156–7.
70. Ibid, p. 172.
71. Ibid, p. 307.
72. Ian Watt, *The Rise of the Novel: Studies in Defoe, Richardson, and Fielding*, London: Chatto & Windus, 1957, p. 57.

73. G. W. F. Hegel, *Phenomenology of the Spirit*, 1807; references to translation by A. V. Miller, Oxford University Press, 1977, p. 478.
74. Samuel Richardson, *Clarissa*, 1740, here, London: Everyman, 1962, p. 118.
75. Rita Goldberg, *Sex and Enlightenment*, Cambridge University Press, 1984, p. 159.
76. Ibid, p. 23.
77. See Keith Thomas 'Women and the Civil War Sects', *Past and Present*, 13 (1958), pp. 42–57.

3 'The Social', 'Woman', and Sociological Feminism

1. Madame de Staël, *De La Littérature, Considerée dans ses rapports avec les institutions sociales*, 1800 (An. 8). References here are to the 2nd edition, *The Influence of Literature upon Society*, London, 1812, pp. 161–2.
2. Ibid, p. 165.
3. Ibid, p. 168.
4. Ibid, pp. 162–3.
5. John Stuart Mill, *The Subjection of Women*, 1869, London: Virago, 1983, pp. 38–9.
6. Harriet Taylor, 'The Enfranchisement of Women', *Westminster Review*, London, July 1851, p. 13.
7. Jacques Derrida, 'The Ends of Man', *Philosophy and Phenomenological Research*, vol. 30, 1969, pp. 31–57.
8. John Millar, *Observation concerning the distinction of ranks in society*, Edinburgh, 1771. Subsequently, *The origin of the distinction of ranks*, Edinburgh: W. Blackwood, 1806.
9. François Quesnay, 'Tableau Economique', 1st edition, Versailles, Dec. 1758. See discussions by Harold Benenson, 'The Origins of the Concept of Class and Gender Ideology', and 'The Impact of Political Economic Thought on the Analysis of Women's Subordination', Dept. of Sociology, Sarah Lawrence College, New York, 1985 and 1987.
10. Auguste Comte, *A General View of Positivism* (trans.) London: Routledge & Kegan Paul, 1907, pp. 1–7.
11. Ibid, pp. 1–7.
12. Harriet Martineau, *The positive philosophy of Auguste Comte*, freely translated and condensed by Harriet Martineau, London: J. Chapman, 1853.
13. Jeffrey Minson, 'Administrative Amnesia', paper to Law and Society Conference, Macquarie University, Australia, 1984; and see his further discussion of 'the social' in *Genealogies of Morals: Nietzsche, Foucault, Donzelot and the Eccentricity of Ethics*, London: Macmillan, 1986.
14. Plato, the *Timaeus*, 52, quotation as translated by Julia Kristeva in

'Women's Time', translated by Alice Jardine, *Signs, A Journal of Women in Culture and Society*, vol. 7, no. 1, 1981, pp. 13–35.

15. Thus, for instance, Maud Pember Reeves, *Round About a Pound a Week*, London: G. Bell & Sons Ltd, 1913, and Virago, 1979; and Margaret Llewelyn Davies (ed.), *Maternity; Letters from Working Women*, London: G. Bell & Sons Ltd, 1915, and Virago, 1978; and by the same editor, *Life as We Have Known It*, London: Hogarth Press, 1931, and Virago, 1977.

16. See, for instance, Peter Clarke, *Liberals and Social Democrats*, Cambridge University Press, 1978.

17. Transactions of the National Association for the Promotion of Social Science, vol. 1, London, 1858, introductory page xxv.

18. Ibid, p. xxv.

19. Ibid, p. xxxi.

20. Louisa Twining, 'Objects and Aims of the Workhouse Visiting Society', in ibid, p. 671.

21. Mary-Anne Baines, 'The Ladies National Association for the Diffusion of Sanitary Knowledge' in ibid, p. 531.

22. Ibid, p. 531.

23. *Social Science*, the Journal of the National Association for the Promotion of Social Science, London, vol. 1, 1866, p. 272.

24. 'Social Science' in *Blackwood's Magazine*, vol. 90, Edinburgh, July–December, 1861, pp. 463–78, p. 468.

25. Ibid, p. 470.

26. *Social Science*, London, vol. 1, no. 4, 21 Dec. 1866.

27. Mabel Atkinson, *The Economic Foundations of the Women's Movement*, Fabian Tract no. 175, London, June 1914, p. 199.

28. The Committee appointed by the Local Government Board under the chairmanship of Sir John Tudor Walters, to report on working-class housing to be built with government aid: Cd. 9191, London, 1918.

29. See Denise Riley, *War in the Nursery: Theories of the Child and Mother*, London: Virago, 1983, pp. 184–96.

30. Alva Myrdal, *Nation and Family*, London: Kegan Paul, Trench, Trubner & Co, 1945, p. 121.

31. May Sinclair, *The Tree of Heaven*, London: Macmillan, 1917, p. 124.

32. Richard Aldington, *Death of a Hero*, London: Chatto & Windus, 1929, p. 257.

33. Virginia Woolf, *Three Guineas*, London: Hogarth, 1938, p. 101.

34. Ibid, p. 102.

35. Winifred Holtby, 'Feminism Divided', *Time and Tide*, 8 August 1924; reprinted in *Testament of a Generation: The Journalism of Vera Brittain and Winifred Holtby*, edited by P. Berry and A. Bishop, London: Virago, 1985, p. 48.

36. Vera Brittain, 'Why Feminism Lives', pamphlet published by the Six Point Group in 1927, reprinted in *Testament of a Generation*, p. 99.

37. Ibid, p. 99.

38. Vera Brittain, 'Mrs. Pankhurst and the Older Feminists', *Manches-*

ter Guardian, 20 June 1928; reprinted in *Testament of a Generation*, p. 101.

39. Winifred Holtby, in the *Clarion*, 24 March 1934; reprinted in *Testament of a Generation*, p. 84.
40. Ibid, p. 86.
41. Mrs C. S. (Dorothy) Peel, *The Labour Saving House*, London, 1917.
42. For instance, Dora Russell, *Hypatia*, London: Kegan Paul, Trench, Trubner & Co. Ltd, 1925; and Naomi Mitchison, *Comments on Birth Control*, London: Faber & Faber, 1930.
43. Virginia Woolf, *A Room of One's Own*, London: Hogarth, 1929, p. 91.
44. Ibid, p. 96.
45. Ibid, p. 103.
46. Ibid, p. 107.
47. Ibid, p. 108.
48. Ibid, p. 118.
49. Ibid, p. 100.
50. Simone de Beauvoir, *The Second Sex*, trans. H. Parshley, London: Jonathan Cape, 1953; and reprinted by Penguin, 1972, p. 726.
51. See Mary Wollstonecraft, *A Vindication of the Rights of Woman*, London, 1792: Penguin, 1982, p. 142.
52. See also Sally Alexander's discussion in 'Women, Class, and Sexual Differences in the 1830s and 1840s; some reflections on the writing of a feminist history', *History Workshop*, London, Spring 1984, pp. 125–49.

4 The Womanly Vote

1. Olympe de Gouges, *Les Droits de la Femme*, Paris, n.d. (1791), and see *Women in Revolutionary Paris, 1789–1795, Selected Documents*, trans. with notes and commentary by D. G. Levy, H. B. Applewhite and M. D. Johnson, Chicago: University of Illinois Press, 1979.
2. Anon., *Women's Rights and Duties*, London, 1840; excerpted in Patricia Hollis, *Women in Public; The Women's Movement 1850–1900*, London: George Allen & Unwin, 1979, p. 292. This is a most useful selection of documents, to which I refer where possible, for ease of access.
3. This, and the immediately following phrases: ibid, and in Hollis, p. 292.
4. 'Objections to Woman Suffrage', speech to the Electoral Reform Conference, London, 1874: in Hollis, p. 307.
5. 'Present Aspect of Woman's Suffrage Considered', speech to the London National Society for Women's Suffrage, 1877: in Hollis, p. 311.

6. Speech on Women's Disabilities Bill to the House of Commons, Hansard, 3 May 1871: in Hollis, p. 305.
7. Ibid, pp. 305–6.
8. Mrs Humphrey Ward *et al.*, 'An appeal against female suffrage', *The Nineteenth Century*, June 1889: and in Hollis, p. 326.
9. Ibid, p. 325.
10. Ibid, p. 325.
11. Ibid, p. 325.
12. W. E. Gladstone, letter to Mr Samuel Smith, 11 April 1892: in Hollis, p. 319.
13. J. S. Mill, Speech to the House of Commons, Hansard, 20 May 1867: in Hollis, p. 300.
14. Ibid, pp. 300–1.
15. Ibid, p. 301.
16. Mrs Hugo Reid, *A Plea for Women*, London, 1843, p. 64: in Hollis, p. 293.
17. Gladstone's letter, as above: in Hollis, p. 320.
18. In *Fraser's Magazine*, vol. 78, 1868: in Hollis, p. 294.
19. 'Present Aspect of Woman's Suffrage Considered', speech as above: in Hollis, p. 310.
20. Millicent Garrett Fawcett, 'Female Suffrage: a reply', *The Nineteenth Century*, July 1889: in Hollis, p. 331.
21. J. S. Mill, Speech to the House of Commons, Hansard, 20 May 1867: in Hollis, p. 229.
22. Ibid, p. 229.
23. Mr Beresford Hope, Speech in the Debate on the Women's Disabilities Bill, House of Commons, Hansard, 3 May 1871: in Hollis, p. 305.
24. Ibid, p. 306.
25. 'An appeal against female suffrage', as above: in Hollis, p. 324.
26. Ibid, p. 324.
27. Arabella Shore, 'Present Aspect of Woman's Suffrage Considered', as above: in Hollis, p. 309.
28. Ibid, p. 310.
29. 'An appeal against female suffrage', as above: in Hollis, p. 323.
30. Ibid, p. 323.
31. Ibid, p. 323.
32. Harriet Taylor, 'Enfranchisement of women', *Westminster Review*, vol. 55, London, 1851: in Hollis, p. 293.
33. Barbara Leigh Smith Bodichon, *Reasons For and Against the Enfranchisement of Women*, London, 1866: in Hollis, p. 295.
34. J. S. Mill, Speech to the House of Commons, Hansard, 20 May 1867: in Hollis, p. 298.
35. Ibid, p. 298.
36. 'The emancipation of women', editorial in the *Westminster Review*, vol. 128, 1887: in Hollis, p. 329.
37. 'An appeal against female suffrage', as above: in Hollis, pp. 322–3.
38. Ibid, p. 324.
39. Ibid, p. 324.

40. W. E. Gladstone, Letter to Mr Samuel Smith, 11 April 1892: in Hollis, p. 320.
41. J. S. Mill, as above: Hollis, p. 301.
42. Ibid, p. 300.
43. Ibid, p. 302.
44. Ibid, p. 304.
45. Captain Maxse, 'Objections to Women's Suffrage', Speech to the Electoral Reform Conference, 1874: in Hollis, p. 307.
46. Ibid, p. 307.
47. Ibid, p. 308.
48. Ibid, p. 308.
49. Arabella Shore, 'Present Aspect of Woman's Suffrage Considered', as above: in Hollis, p. 310.
50. Ibid, p. 311.
51. Ibid, p. 313.
52. See Olive Banks, *Faces of Feminism*, Oxford: Martin Robertson, 1981, p. 125.
53. Frank Prochaska, *Women and Philanthropy in Nineteenth Century England*, Oxford: Oxford University Press, 1980, p. 229.
54. Ibid, p. 229.
55. Martin Pugh, 'Politicians and the Woman's Vote, 1914–1918', *History*, October 1974, p. 368. See also his *Women's Suffrage in Britain 1867–1928*, London: Historical Association, 1980.
56. Brian Harrison, *Separate Spheres: The Opposition to Women's Suffrage in Britain*, London: Croom Helm, 1978, pp. 60–64.
57. Ibid, p. 51.
58. Ibid, pp. 133–6.
59. Ernest Belfort Bax, *The Fraud of Feminism*, London, 1913, p. 76.
60. Quoted in Brian Harrison, *Separate Spheres*, as above, p. 247.
61. See the discussion in Harrison, pp. 228–38.

5 Bodies, Identities, Feminisms

1. Donna Haraway, 'A Manifesto for Cyborgs: Science, Technology and Socialist Feminism in the 1980s', *Socialist Review*, 80, vol. 15, no. 2, March–April, 1985, p. 92.
2. Ibid, p. 95.
3. Simone de Beauvoir, *Le Deuxième Sexe, 1949: The Second Sex*, transl. by H. Parshley, London: Jonathan Cape, 1953, p. 84.
4. Elizabeth Gross, 'Philosophy, subjectivity, and the body: Kristeva and Irigaray', in Carole Pateman and Elizabeth Gross (eds), *Feminist Challenges: Social and Political Theory*, Sydney: Allen & Unwin, 1986, p. 139.
5. See Edward Shorter, *A History of Women's Bodies*, New York: Basic Books, 1982.

6. Sebastiano Timpanaro, *On Materialism*, London: New Left Books, 1975.

7. Michel Foucault, *The History of Sexuality* – Volume 1: An Introduction, trans. R. Hurley, London: Allen Lane, 1979.

8. Michel Foucault, 'Nietzsche, Genealogy, History', in *Language, Counter-Memory, Practice: Selected Essays and Interviews*, Donald F. Bouchard and Sherry Simon (eds and transl.), Ithaca: Cornell University Press, 1977, p. 148.

9. Ibid, p. 153.

10. Elizabeth Gross, 'Philosophy, subjectivity, and the body: Kristeva and Irigaray' (as above), p. 142.

11. William Empson, *The Structure of Complex Words*, London, 1951, p. 29.

12. Ibid, p. 39.

13. Ibid: see Empson's discussion of I. A. Richards, *The Philosophy of Rhetoric*.

14. Julia Kristeva, 'Le temps des femmes', transl. as 'Women's Time' by Alice Jardine and Harry Blake, *Signs*, vol. 7:1, Autumn, 1981, p. 35.

15. Ibid, p. 17.

16. Ibid, p. 19.

17. Ibid, p. 20.

18. Ibid, p. 33.

19. Ibid, p. 34.

20. Ibid, p. 34.

21. Ibid, p. 35.

22. Winifred Holtby, 'Feminism Divided', *Yorkshire Post*, 26 July 1926, in *Testament of a Generation: The Journalism of Vera Brittain and Winifred Holtby*, (eds and intro.) Paul Berry and Alan Bishop, London: Virago, 1985, p. 48.

23. See Joan Scott, 'The Sears Case', in *Gender and The Politics of History*, New York: Columbia University Press, forthcoming, 1988.

24. Maurice Merleau-Ponty, *The Phenomenology of Perception*, trans. Colin Smith, London: Routledge & Kegan Paul, 1962, p. 171.

Selective Bibliography

(Fuller bibliographical information is given in the chapter notes.)

ANON., *An Essay in Defence of the Female Sex*, London, 1696.

ANON., *Women's Rights and Duties*, London, 1840.

ALDINGTON, R., *Death of a Hero*, London, 1929.

ALEXANDER, S., 'Women, Class, and Sexual Differences in the 1830s and 1840s: some reflections on the writing of a feminist history', *History Workshop*, Spring 1984.

ANGER, J., 'Jane Anger her Protection for Women . . .', in J. Goulianos (ed.), *By a Woman Writt, Literature from Six Centuries By and About Women*, Baltimore, 1974.

ASTELL, M., *Reflections upon Marriage*, London, 1700.

ASTELL, M., *A Serious Proposal to the Ladies, for the Advancement of their True and Greatest Interest*, London, 1694.

ATKINSON, M., *The Economic Foundations of the Women's Movement*, London, 1914.

BANKS, O., *Faces of Feminism*, Oxford, 1981.

BAX, E. B., *The Fraud of Feminism*, London, 1913.

BENENSON, H., 'The Origins of the Concept of Class and Gender Ideology', Dept. of Sociology, Sarah Lawrence College, New York, 1985.

BENENSON, H., 'The Impact of Political Economic Thought on the Analysis of Women's Subordination', Dept. of Sociology, Sarah Lawrence College, New York, 1987.

BERRY, P. and BISHOP, A. (eds), *Testament of a Generation: The Journalism of Vera Brittain and Winifred Holtby*, London, 1985.

Blackwood's Magazine, vol. 90, 1861.

BLAKE, W., *The Song of Los*, 1795.

BODICHON, B. L. S., *Reasons For and Against the Enfranchisement of Women*, London, 1866.

CLARKE, P., *Liberals and Social Democrats*, Cambridge, 1978.

COMTE, A., *A General View of Positivism*, London, 1907.

DAVIES, M. L. (ed.), *Life as We Have Known It (1931)*, London, 1977.

DAVIES, M. L. (ed.), *Maternity: Letters from Working Women (1915)*, London 1978.

BEAUVOIR, S de, *The Second Sex*, trans. H. Parshley London, 1953.

DRONKE, P., *Women Writers of the Middle Ages*, Cambridge, 1984.

EMPSON, W., *The Structure of Complex Words*, London, 1951.

FAWCETT, M.G., 'Female Suffrage: a reply', *The Nineteenth Century*, 1889.

FOUCAULT, M., *The History of Sexuality* – Volume 1: An Introduction, trans. R. Hurley, London, 1979.

FOUCAULT, M., 'Nietzsche, Genealogy, History', in D. F. Bouchard and

S. Simon (eds and trans.), *Language, Counter-Memory, Practice; Selected Essays and Interviews*, Ithaca, 1977.

GOLDBERG, R., *Sex and Enlightenment*, Cambridge, 1984.

GOUGES, O de, *Les Droits de la Femme*, Paris, 1791.

GROSS, E., 'Philosophy, subjectivity and the body: Kristeva and Irigaray', in C. Pateman and E. Gross (eds), *Feminist Challenges: Social and Political Theory*, Sydney, 1986.

HARAWAY, D., 'A Manifesto for Cyborgs: Science, Technology and Socialist Feminism in the 1980s', *Socialist Review*, 80, 1985.

HARRISON, B., *Separate Spheres: The Opposition to Women's Suffrage in Britain*, London, 1978.

HEGEL, G. W. F., *Phenomenology of the Spirit* (1807), trans. A. V. Miller, Oxford, 1977.

HOLLIS, P., *Women in Public: The Women's Movement 1850–1900*, London, 1979.

KLEY, D. van, *The Jansenists and the Expulsion of the Jesuits from France, 1757–1765*, New Haven, 1975.

KRISTEVA, J., 'Le temps des femmes', A. Jardine and H. Blake (trans.), *Signs*, 7, 1981.

LEVY, D. G., APPLEWHITE, H. B. and JOHNSON, M. D., *Women in Revolutionary Paris, 1789–1795*, Chicago, 1979.

LLOYD, G., *The Man of Reason; 'Male' and 'Female' in Western Philosophy*, London, 1984.

MACLEAN I., *The Renaissance Notion of Woman: a study in the fortunes of scholasticism and medical science in European intellectual life*, Cambridge, 1980.

MARTINEAU, H., *The Positive Philosophy of Auguste Comte*, London, 1853.

MCINTYRE, A., *A Short History of Ethics*, London, 1967.

MERLEAU-PONTY, M., *The Phenomenology of Perception*, trans. C. Smith, London, 1962.

MILL, J. S., *The Subjection of Women* (1869), London, 1983.

MILLAR, J., *Observation concerning the distinction of ranks in society*, Edinburgh, 1771; subsequently, *The origin of the distinction of ranks*, Edinburgh, 1806.

MINSON, J., 'Administrative Amnesia,' paper, Law and Society Conference, Macquarie University, Australia, 1984.

MINSON, J., *Genealogies of Morals: Nietzsche, Foucault, Donzelot and the Eccentricity of Ethics*, London, 1986.

MITCHELL, J. and Rose, J. (eds), *Feminine Sexuality, Jacques Lacan and the École Freudienne*, London, 1982.

MITCHISON, N., *Comments on Birth Control*, London, 1930.

MYRDAL, A., *Nation and Family*, London, 1945.

NEWCASTLE, Margaret Lucas Cavendish, Duchess of, *Divers Orations*, London, 1662.

NEWCASTLE, Margaret Lucas Cavendish, Duchess of, *A Treasure of Knowledge, OR, The Female Oracle*: in A. NICOL, *Poems on Several Subjects*, Edinburgh, 1766.

NICOL, A., *Poems on Several Subjects*, Edinburgh, 1766.

PATEMAN, C. and GROSS, E. (eds), *Feminist Challenges: Social and Political Theory*, Sydney, 1986.

PROCHASKA, F., *Women and Philanthropy in Nineteenth Century England*, Oxford, 1980.

PUGH, M., 'Politicians and the Woman's Vote, 1914–1918', *History*, 1974.

PUGH, M., 'Women's Suffrage in Britain 1867–1928', *Historical Association*, 1980.

QUESNAY, F., 'Tableau Economique', Versailles, 1758.

REEVES, M. P., *Round About a Pound a Week* (1913), London, 1979.

REID, MRS H., *A Plea for Women*, London, 1843.

RICHARDSON, S., *Clarissa*, (1740), Everyman edn, London, 1962.

RIDING, L., *The Poems of Laura Riding*, 1938.

RILEY, D., *War in the Nursery: Theories of the Child and Mother*, London, 1983.

ROUSSEAU, J. J., *Émile, ou de l'Education* (1762, 1780) trans. (Everyman edn) London, 1905.

ROUSSEAU, J. J., *La Nouvelle Héloise* (1761), trans. W. Kenrick, *Eloisa*, 1776.

RUSSELL, D., *Hypatia*, London, 1925.

SCOTT, J. W., 'The Sears Case', *Gender and the Politics of History*, New York (forthcoming), 1988.

SCOTT, J. W., "'L'Ouvrière! Mot Impie, Sordide . . .'': Women Workers in the Discourse of French Political Economy (1840–1860)', in P. Joyce (ed.), *The Historical Meanings of Work*, Cambridge, 1987.

SEGAL, L., *Is the Future Female? Troubled Thoughts on Contemporary Feminism*, London, 1987.

SHAKESPEARE, W., *Othello*, 1622.

SINCLAIR, M., *The Tree of Heaven*, London, 1917.

Social Science, Vol. 1, London, 1866.

STAËL, MADAME DE, *De La Littérature, consideeré dans ses rapports avec les institutions sociales* (1800); 2nd edn, *The Influence of Literature upon Society*, London, 1812.

STEIN, G., Libretto for *The Mother of us All*, an operetta by V. Thomson, 1947.

TAYLOR, H., 'The Enfranchisement of Women', *Westminster Review*, 55, 1851.

THOMAS, K., 'Women and the Civil War Sects', *Past and Present*, 13, 1958.

THOMPSON, E. P., *The Poverty of Theory, or An Orrery of Errors*, London, 1978.

Transactions of the National Association for the Promotion of Social Science, vol. 1, London, 1858.

WARD, MRS H., 'An appeal against female suffrage', *The Nineteenth Century*, 1889.

WATT, I., *The Rise of the Novel: Studies in Defoe, Richardson, and Fielding*, London, 1957.

WOLLSTONECRAFT, M., *A Vindication of the Rights of Women* (1792). Harmondsworth, 1982.

WOOLF, V., *A Room of One's Own*, London, 1929.

WOOLF, V., *Three Guineas*, London, 1938.